TAKE THE LEAP

What It Really Means to Be Psychic

MICHELLE A. BELTRAN

BALBOA.
PRESS

A DIVISION OF HAY HOUSE

Balboa Press books may be ordered through booksellers or by contacting:

Balboa Press
A Division of Hay House
1663 Liberty Drive
Bloomington, IN 47403
www.balboapress.com
1 (877) 407-4847

Because of the dynamic nature of the Internet, any web addresses or links contained in this book may have changed since publication and may no longer be valid. The views expressed in this work are solely those of the author and do not necessarily reflect the views of the publisher, and the publisher hereby disclaims any responsibility for them.

The author of this book does not dispense medical advice or prescribe the use of any technique as a form of treatment for physical, emotional, or medical problems without the advice of a physician, either directly or indirectly. The intent of the author is only to offer information of a general nature to help you in your quest for emotional and spiritual well-being. In the event you use any of the information in this book for yourself, which is your constitutional right, the author and the publisher assume no responsibility for your actions.

Any people depicted in stock imagery provided by Thinkstock are models, and such images are being used for illustrative purposes only.
Certain stock imagery © Thinkstock.

Print information available on the last page.

ISBN: 978-1-5043-3999-5 (sc)
ISBN: 978-1-5043-4001-4 (hc)
ISBN: 978-1-5043-4000-7 (e)

Library of Congress Control Number: 2015914204

Balboa Press rev. date: 08/28/2015

This book is dedicated to my grandmothers: Adeline (Nini), for being with me every step of the way, even after her last breath; and Matilda (Tillie), for her Mother Teresa–like work in this lifetime.

CONTENTS

ACKNOWLEDGMENTS

Writing a book is like the peloton. It is a collaboration of a team traversing obstacles, gaining momentum, and being keenly aware. It is a team being responsive to every turn and switchback and moving forward in a collective, dynamic rhythm.

With deepest gratitude, I thank the following people, with whom I am blessed to have crossed the finish line:

To my teachers and coaches, thank you, thank you, thank you.

To my many students and clients, from whom I learned so much and who inspired this book into being.

To my family and friends, who believed in me.

To the dedicated group of savvy professionals who walked alongside me on this writing journey.

And to you, for allowing this book to find its way into your hands.

CHAPTER 1

MY STORY

Some years ago, I embarked on the journey of a lifetime—or maybe several lifetimes. I had lived a fairly nomadic professional life, moving from one career or enthusiasm to another. I'd been in the air force, worked as a probation officer, taught young people, and been a professional cyclist. Once, when I was working as a probation officer, my chief described my life as being "rich with escapades." She wasn't entirely wrong, and in spite of the fact that the description appeared accurate, it was not how I would have described it. I had an overwhelming sense—a primordial urging—that something was not right, that there must be more to life than this seemingly fortunate life I was leading.

I remember sitting in my office, comfortably employed with the state in a position many would have been thrilled to hold, knowing I was not living up to my potential. Life should be engaging, passion-filled, and stimulating. That realization prompted a couple of questions I had never asked myself before: What exactly is my potential? How do I go about pursuing it?

These questions brought awareness that the only way to complete fulfillment was to embrace the thing I had inwardly desired my entire life—the development of my mind, my consciousness, my inner leanings, and my psychic propensities.

Once I committed myself to this journey of self-discovery, I focused all my attention on growing an awareness of my higher self, my connections with the universe, and the psychic abilities I had overlooked and ignored. I haven't looked back since that day.

I began formal psychic training at the Chico Psychic Institute. Later, I studied at the Reno Psychic Institute in Reno, Nevada. Shortly thereafter, I discovered mediumship abilities and studied at Mystic Shift Mediumship School. Each class and each new revelation served to kindle my excitement and energy for more. My skills were expanding, and my abilities were blossoming and developing. I no longer had superficial ideas about the psychic realm and just how psychic development happens. I studied and read everything I could and began practicing my innate abilities earnestly and sincerely. Several psychic practices caught my interest, but I was most intrigued by the practice of controlled remote viewing, what I now call Distant Sensing.

Like anyone who embarks on this lifestyle quickly discerns, I had an inclination for practices for which I later learned I had a talent. I soon discovered that practice was Distant Sensing. I found it captivating and fascinating. With fervor, I sought out expert guidance from Dr. Paul H. Smith, one of the longest-serving remote viewers in the Star Gate psychic military espionage program. Distant Sensing was a scientific connection to a profession—psychic examination—that I knew to be valid but others found hard to trust. I believed that if the Central Intelligence Agency found value and significance in psychic research, it was possible to change the public's negative perceptions and prejudices.

If you're reading this book, you must be curious about the powers of the mind. Like me, you may have the feeling there is more to life than can be explained by our physical experience of the world. Quoted in the book *The Joy of Kindness* by Robert Furey, I thoroughly believe what the French philosopher and Jesuit priest, Pierre Teilhard de Chardin, wrote about the reality of living: "We are not human beings having a spiritual experience. We are spiritual beings having a human experience."

It didn't take long before I teamed up with Deborah King, an internationally known life coach and alternative healer, and things changed even more dramatically. Her biography—a study in overcoming obstacles, moving on to success, and the recounting of her quest for self-knowledge—resonated with me. It was her life story that led me to realize the importance and impact of reaching one's higher self. Deborah helped me orient my teaching and focus my objectives. I soon opened my own practice and currently work to help thousands who need answers to life's big questions. My practice consists of mediumship, controlled remote viewing (Distant Sensing), psychic readings, and intuitive life coaching. It is my hope that you will dive deeply into exploring your own higher self and give credit to your special psychic callings.

CHAPTER 2

TAKE THE LEAP: WHAT IT REALLY MEANS TO BE PSYCHIC

The steps we take on life's journey are fraught with ups and downs, misconceptions and falsehoods, unexpected realizations and unprecedented understandings. Life is learning. Even our ability to observe firsthand events correctly is impacted by the inability of our brains to record more than five specific facts at one time. The other facts—rightly or wrongly remembered—are filtered out of our recollection. Our observations are also influenced by our worldview and past influences, not actual facts. The realm of psychic and otherworldly happenings, like our observations, can't be definitively defined. But in spite of that, the world of psychic phenomena has thousands of followers, and the people who believe in an active, unseen world practice its teachings.

What we do know about this area of life is that such belief structures are part of our culture. The world of active spirituality, of psychic seeing, mediumship, and other psychic modalities, is growing. Just as many people are interested in religious principles and inspirations, many are interested in the mysterious realm of the supernatural. In the past, people thought something was wrong with anyone who thought about psychic or spiritual matters. Now people are curious. They are in the midst of reconsidering any information they've learned about the universe and the world of the unseen. There is a new wave of investigation into such things as intuition, hunches, instinct, unusual awareness, and the possibility of a sixth sense.

Malcolm Gladwell, in his book *Blink: The Power of Thinking without Thinking* takes a long, hard look at the power and presence of the seldom-understood phenomenon we call intuition. We can't conclusively explain intuition, but researchers like Gladwell have taken a stab at it. His argument suggests our mental processes work quickly and automatically, using an overabundance of information acquired over a lifetime. He puts forth a theory that expert judgment and instantaneous decisions are often accurate without the benefit of extensive knowledge. He also looks into factors that prevent us from using our intuition knowingly and investigates the influences that appear to destroy this mechanism of human intuition.

Others also believe intuition is the result of a lifetime of experiences—an exposure to information residing in our subconscious until the accumulation of that information can be used. These people believe our minds have the ability to archive all types of information we don't log in on a conscious level. They believe we pick up information subconsciously, never really comprehending it—body language, tone of voice, a particular look, or something out of place—and this is the root of intuition.

To others, however, intuition is a knowing or sensing that comes from within because we are a part of a universal mind, and it comes without the benefit of rational explanation. They believe intuition is an unnamed something that operates beneath our layers of logic, something that works as our conscious and unconscious minds communicate in unexpected ways, an unconscious reasoning that propels us to do things without telling us why or how. In the book *Steve Jobs*, by Walter Isaacson, Jobs, an inventor and pioneer of the computer revolution, called intuition, "more powerful than intellect." Intuition, for both camps, is the sum of our intellectual ability, acquired knowledge, past experiences, and sensory perceptions. For some, it also includes psychic input.

Whatever intuition is, it is not instinct. Instinct is an internally driven, fixed pattern of behavior exhibited in animals in response to a specific stimulus. It is an inborn impulse, a motivation to action. Salmon swim upstream and fight strong river currents in response to a compulsion to return to their birthplaces and spawn a new generation. Salmon do this in response to instinct, not intuition. Intuition is an experience unique to humans.

Intuition not only uses our mental senses to inform us, but it also uses our bodies to send us unique messages. You may have heard it said, "He makes the hairs on the back of my neck stand up." That is intuition using your physical body to signal something may be wrong or needs your attention. It may be telling you the person or situation in question is unsafe. Intuition might be a tingle, a feeling in your stomach, or an unsettling emotion. It is intuition sending you a message.

To people like Gladwell, intuition and foreknowledge are scientific in nature. To those who believe in otherworldly existences, it is spiritual. While it may seem incompatible to forge a link between the common, everyday experiences of intuition and the trained and developed powers of a psychic, psychics tell us intuition is the foundation upon which psychic abilities are built.

Regardless of where the truth lies on this issue, our culture actively encourages us to rely on rational judgment as the only true expression of reality. We know, however, that purely rational assessments aren't always accurate. We have all experienced instances where emotional input has aided in the discovery of a truth or the reality of an event or situation. Intuition is a worthwhile guide for evaluating situations and informing decisions. It has the ability to take us to unexpected destinations without the benefit of logic.

If you have ever had a gut feeling that turned out to be true or had a sudden impulse to do or not do something but later discovered you should have listened, you were using the intuitive insights with which we are all endowed. Given that intuition lives in the realm of the unexplained, you may be able to conclude (in a broad sense) that you already have the foundation for acquiring psychic abilities. All individuals are born with a tendency toward a psychic mind, whether they know it or not or believe it or not. Psychic abilities are an integral and important part (albeit a small part) of intuition.

It is quite possible for individuals to make the conscious decision to develop, rekindle, or magnify the powers of their intuitive voices, their psychic minds. This book is written to discuss what it means to be psychic. The path to the supernatural world of the psychic begins by expanding and fine-tuning intuition and then paying close attention to the seen and unseen worlds that surround us. Wayne Dyer, internationally renowned author and speaker on the topics of self-development and spiritual growth, like many in his field, believes current scientific investigation around the mysteries of matter and energy proves it is quite possible there is more beyond what our logical minds can consider.

For many, religion is the answer to universal truth and a connection with supreme intelligence. Current statistics report a majority of Americans believe angels and demons are active in the world. Eighty percent believe miracles happen, and 92 percent believe in God. To others, cultivating and establishing psychic abilities will aid in a search for the power of a universal mind and a universal spirit that unifies us all.

The acquisition of psychic abilities is not simply the pursuit of a psychic mind. It is more about embarking on a journey of self-discovery to awaken an innate desire to understand the universe and the unseen world. It is not a question of being more intuitive than anyone else, and it is not a question of being endowed with more psychic abilities than anyone else. It is only about you and whether or not you want to engage in an exploration of the spirit realm or acquire psychic abilities by becoming familiar with the practices of the psychic world.

CHAPTER 3

WHO OR WHAT IS A PSYCHIC

Apsychic is a person who recognizes the supernatural capabilities of the mind and works to expand his or her skills and develop those abilities lying outside the realm of physical science or earthly understanding—powers and abilities that function outside the domain of natural laws. Psychic abilities involve skills to interpret, manipulate, and report on events and information that can't be acquired within the sphere of physical science.

Psychics deal with things pertaining to the human soul and mind. They engage in powers relating to spiritual forces, the immaterial, and the influences of universal energy. Such efforts result in the development of insights and abilities, like telepathy and clairvoyance. People who have worked at developing their psychic abilities will find they become proficient in one or several of the activities commonly referred to as mediumship, clairvoyance, telepathy, mind reading, ESP, palmistry, and other aids to spiritual exploration.

Psychic abilities can be acquired by anyone who takes the time and makes the effort to study and learn. It isn't necessary to be highly evolved or believe in psychic inclinations that may have occurred in childhood. Everyone has psychic potential, but their abilities often remain inactive until something triggers them into action. Psychic ability, like any skill, develops only when wanted and practiced. It fades when it is neglected.

Scientific proof that psychic powers exist is gaining ground. Thousands practice the art, and thousands more believe. Physicist and author, Russell Targ, states in his book *The Reality of ESP: A Physicist's Proof of Psychic Abilities* the scientific evidence that we all possess psychic abilities is "… now overwhelming and modern physics has the means and tools to embrace it." Mediums and psychics have been relaying messages and conducting readings for thousands of years. Even Solomon sought the advice of a spiritualist and received it, although he acted against God's instructions. The result was he obtained information about the outcome of an upcoming battle.

Today, there are a larger number of spiritualists practicing than ever before, and there is a greater acceptance of spiritual expressions. Seventy-two percent of all Americans describe themselves as *spiritual but not religious*. Individuals like Oprah Winfrey, Alice Walker, Richard Bach, Elizabeth Gilbert, Louise Hay, Neale Donald Walsh, and Iyanla Vanzant are some of those Americans.

Psychic practices are no longer considered taboo, and people who side with those beliefs are no longer considered bizarre, creepy, or peculiar. The psychic profession is now accepted. It is a practice that endeavors to uncover an inner view of the soul and the universal connection of souls. Psychics believe since we are all souls and we are all connected, we are all psychic on some level. How adept we become at using those psychic tendencies is up to us; growth takes training.

Training to be a psychic, like the training for any occupation, is necessary. And because you have the power of choice, you can decide to develop your psychic gifts whenever you want and for whatever reason you want. No one, even those in the psychic community, knows for sure or can prove where psychic gifts come from. So it is up to you to trust the process and believe that any psychic power can be acquired.

The psychic community believes spiritual energies are working for the good of humankind—energies that will guide you to the realization of your true spiritual nature and to the highest expression of who you are. They believe that psychic gifts, when used properly, benefit you and do not function to flatter your ego. Psychic practices support identifying the true essence of the soul and illuminate for the world the true nature and meaning of spirituality.

CHAPTER 4

ABOUT BEING A PSYCHIC

The difference between those with psychic Sense-Abilities and those without is simply a matter of training and intention. The mind is not just a function of the body, like an arm or a leg. It is a powerful tool from which we can access the universe and our inner selves. Each of us can learn to stand in our own power, in our own way, and in our own time; psychic training can do all of that.

You see, psychics, and those who are interested in investigating the power of the universe and the unexplainable, share the same characteristics. You've met them. They are people who seem to know what's going to happen before it happens, those who seem to read minds, those who are both cursed and blessed by being highly intuitive. They are people who appear to go about their lives in a different way.

Psychics

- pay particular attention to their inner voices and listen to its urgings;
- pay attention to their bodies and are not afraid to be mystical;
- make time for solitude and take advantage of opportunities to contemplate the mysteries of existence;
- cherish creativity and put time into feeding that creativity;

- observe everything around them and attempt to make sense of what they see. They are drawn to finding the truth in others and in the world; and
- pay attention to their dreams, knowing that truth can be found in the spirit world as well as the physical world.

Sometimes a person will find himself or herself inundated with a strong suspicion of being more intuitive and more introspective than most. It is quite common that a person will come face-to-face with an overwhelming desire to find out what is actually behind what is seemingly unexplainable. Life often changes in an instant, forcing us to adjust to new information and new realities. But our adjustments to those changes are often gradual. Life changes can be like a soft, sloping curve on which we find ourselves on the other side of a theory, without having recognized the forces that moved us there.

Everything begins with feelings and occurrences you know are more than mere coincidence—strange and undeniable *knowings* you find impossible to ignore. You may have experienced a strong urge to call a relative, only to find out that you were needed at that very moment. Experiences like these happen more often to you than to others. During those times, acting on those feelings or urges—not logic—produces positive results. There may be times you suspect there is something beyond what's called *reality*, something residing in the world of the paranormal.

It is said that psychic connections are made when a person picks up information in an uncommon way or from an unusual source. Psychic connections are said to be in play when a person acquires knowledge he or she could not have known—information emanating from a source outside of individual understanding, separate from any previous experiences or prior knowledge. While there is no scientific proof that these occurrences are psychic in nature, science has yet to explain them. Any psychic will attest that the proof is in the pudding.

He or she has seen it and knows that such information comes directly from the universal mind, the higher self, and/or vibrations sent by other souls— the universal matrix. Psychics believe paranormal principles are the explanation.

Numerous techniques exist by which a person can investigate these mysteries. The investigations center entirely on different psychic practices and specialties psychics pursue. A majority of individuals believe intuition gives us the same information that comes from logical evaluation, personal experience, learned knowledge, and educated conclusions. However, psychics believe that they not only have access to information intuition provides, but that they have the benefit of information that has been passed down from the universe for millennia. They believe information is accessible at the behest of the universal mind and often available through a connection with deceased souls residing in a different reality. Psychics tune into higher sources from outside the human intellect, beyond intuition and learning.

Tuning into higher sources of information begins when individuals aggressively direct their focus on becoming aware of themselves and the world around them. Every day they engage in the paranormal practice of communicating with a higher realm of consciousness, but they are just not aware of doing so.

Once you purposely make it a point to become aware, you will begin to find something else is at work. If you take time to analyze events nonchalantly referred to as coincidences, hunches, urges, or that inner voice, you will come to realize there is more to know about reality. It is even possible you may discover or become aware of the psychic strengths you tend to have. Pay attention to all your hunches, urges, and coincidences, and see if there are deeper messages and/or meanings. In order to stretch your mind's ability to glean more, listen to them.

Psychics look deep into their daily happenings in an effort to make sense of their lives and the roles they play in the universe. Psychics, as a result of centering on their awareness, learn from which specific events they receive most of their insights. This knowledge alerts future psychics to what the essence of their future practices should be.

It is not uncommon for one specific psychic practice (or perhaps several different practices) to resonate solidly with you—techniques that seem more in tune with your soul self than others. All practices are worth exploring in a sincere effort to find your way. Your intention to become aware of your surroundings and yourself will lead you to psychic practices most representing your connection with other dimensions and realities. Those who learn to interpret their urges and those who sincerely attempt to develop their psychic natures will find the following becomes true:

- Your meditations and methods of concentration will strengthen communication between the two hemispheres of your brain. They will enhance the brain's overall activity level and thereby increase brain function.
- The practice of psychic energy will place your mind and body in balance; your overall physical, emotional, and spiritual well-being will improve.
- You will achieve a balanced mind and body connection that will greatly facilitate the reception of psychic messages. It will open the way for clearer thinking and reasoning.
- Your insights involving your inner voice will improve.
- Your senses will become finely tuned (seeing, hearing, smelling, touching, and tasting).
- You will develop a sixth sense, a more intuitive knowing.
- The meditations and other techniques you practice will improve your concentration and awareness.
- You will develop an open pathway to your subconscious.
- You will uncover hidden truths about yourself and situations in your life.

- You will experience enhanced recognition of your inner voice that will help prevent the buildup of negative emotions and thinking.
- You will gain a more complete perspective on issues.
- You will make more integrated decisions.

To embark on the serious development of personal psychic abilities, you must purposely engage in investigating the powers existing within and around you. A psychic pursuit is never a selfish pursuit. The psychic pathway is gentle, powerful, and always noncoercive.

CHAPTER 5

WHAT IT MEANS
TO BE PSYCHIC

Since psychic ability is demonstrated whenever someone picks up information from nontraditional, normally inaccessible sources, one must work to enhance the quality and substance of that information. And since the reception of that information is coming from sources other than a person's intellect or understanding—information beyond his or her own knowledge base, reality, or experience—it is important to learn about those sources and become familiar with the universal mind.

Psychic sensitivities are like receiving a coded message meant specifically for you and understood only by you. It's a kind of awareness that lies outside the realm of the here and now. It is where the presence of otherworldly existences align themselves with your inner being. They do so in order to inform and enlighten you on matters significant to you or others. Psychic awareness deepens the impact of coincidences, hunches, or urges. The universal matrix transmits information across a telepathic thoroughfare that delivers additional information, deeper understandings, and clarification of situations and events. Psychic awareness turns a veiled nudge into a disclosure and an indiscriminate urge into a valuable discovery.

A psychic has access to extensive recorded information held by the universal mind. The psychic's ability to tap into these intense psychic insights is the direct result of establishing a link with the universal mind and its unlimited stores of universal energy. This energy can be tapped by anyone who chooses to make an effort to tune into its subtle vibrations. The role of the psychic is to facilitate his or her connection with that energy and to focus on its workings. The universal mind has chronicled the life of all human beings. It has recorded the events of their lives, their thoughts, their words, and all actions they've taken or ignored. This record is called the universal bank or Akashic Record.

The universal mind is also the keeper of souls, spirits, and the wisdom of the unseen world. Everything in the universe is connected. Everything is connected by universal energy, and since every living thing has a form of consciousness, everything is connected to every other thing by a shared consciousness and a shared energy. People, animals, and plants are all connected to this the universal consciousness and hidden energy permeating the cosmos and tying everything together. This connectedness is the power of the universal mind. And it is the conscientious and determined acquisition of psychic ability that puts anyone in direct contact with the universal mind and its immense power.

Psychic information—the development of your sixth sense— is transmitted through the five senses with which you are already familiar. The spiritual world transmits information through feelings, pictures, sounds, knowing, smelling, and tasting. The spirit, along with other forces in the universal matrix, is the vehicle allowing for spiritual encounters, communications, and experiences. It is how the spiritual world connects directly with the physical world, and psychics are the vessel for those transmissions. While all psychic abilities are natural abilities, development of these abilities must be learned and expanded. Some of these abilities are spontaneous, and others must be learned. One person may inherently be good at one or several psychic modalities, while someone else is good at a completely different set of modalities. Whatever your particular leaning, it will be necessary for you to have an open mind and explore where your particular abilities lie. You will have to look deeper into each instance of intuition or nudging you encounter. You will also have to become accustomed to seeing the deeper messages that present themselves, attuning your mind and thinking to the underlying power driving each event. The ability to effectively connect with the universal mind requires a desire and willingness to connect and develop whatever psychic ability you have and to understand the signals and symbols inherent in any psychic ability.

Everyone is aware of the five senses common to all human beings, senses connecting and informing us of what is going on in the world around us. When these senses are used in conjunction with psychic powers, they are called Sense-Abilities (Clairs). Each modality is connected with the sense it enhances.

The Sense-Abilities are listed here, and although these are the most commonly practiced, there are others that go beyond the scope of this book. They are less prevalent and less frequently practiced. However, they are still considered to be within the realm of psychic phenomena. They, and all the Sense-Abilities, can be experienced at different experiential depths (mental reception levels). While a particular individual may exhibit Visual Receptivity, that same individual may also be able to access a body's overall energy. Each skill is practiced in accordance with a special gift given to the individual. One psychic may be gifted with seeing, and as a result, will specialize in Visual Reception. Another may be gifted with the ability to receive messages through emotions or physical sensation and, therefore, will choose Emotional Reception.

Because our senses are expanded through psychic awareness, it is important to realize that psychic awareness, and its eventual practice, is individualistic. While everyone is born with a deep-seated intuition, each person's path to psychic awareness is unique and valuable. The journey is not about being a psychic, but rather about self-actualization. The extent of involvement in expanding intuitive knowing is paramount to success. It is necessary for translating the information received. Psychic awareness begins with these questions: What do I know about myself? How much more is there to know?

All new endeavors begin by having a clear perception of who you are—your strengths, weaknesses, thoughts, beliefs, motivation, emotions, and desires. Self-actualization is the foundation upon which you build an understanding of people and how they perceive you. It gives you the capacity to recognize where you belong in the universe and what role you are meant to play. Developing self-awareness is important in all aspects of your life here on earth. It means cultivating meaningful relationships and acquiring a sympathetic and empathetic sense for your fellow men and women. When you direct and monitor your behavior to foster positive relationships and work to improve your own shortcomings, you learn to tolerate and forgive the misgivings of others. When you understand the troubles and challenges of your own personality, you learn the meaning of being helpful to others.

Self-awareness will provide you with introspection, to see things the way they really are. It is the first door you must open in order to gauge the truth of things and the responsibilities you hold. It is the first consideration in cultivating a meaningful psychic experience or practice. A meaningful psychic experience will not only work hand-in-hand to help with self-awareness, but it will also provide you with spiritual growth.

It is not easy to know what your unique qualities are and how you fit in this world. It is a life-long challenge to continually keep in touch with who you are, but the challenge is worth it. The clearer picture you have of yourself, the more likely you are to make decisions that serve you well.

Self-awareness is about how to understand your own needs, desires, failings, habits, and everything else that makes you who you are. The more you know about yourself, the more apt you are to effectively adjust to the changes life brings and successfully choose what meets your particular needs.

Embedded in the core of creating a philosophy and set of values to influence how you live your life is self-awareness. It is also the basis of the goals you'll create and the objectives you'll reach. Self-awareness is concerned with collecting data about yourself and making improvements and decisions based on that data.

Requiring more than just an intellectual examination, self-awareness takes the courage to experiment in order to find your own path. It demands that you pay attention to what your feelings are, why you feel the way you do, and what triggers a feeling. The more you pay attention to your emotions and how they work, the better you'll understand why you do the things you do. Self-awareness teaches you empathy, confidence, and discernment about what you want and need. These are all qualities essential for working with others and using your psychic skills productively.

Eckhart Tolle, lauded as one of the most spiritually influential people in the world and author of the bestseller *The Power of Now* once wrote, "To know your self as the being underneath the thinker, the stillness underneath the mental noise, the love and joy underneath the pain, is freedom, salvation, enlightenment."

As you expand your awareness of self and the universe, your knowledge of the universal matrix and otherworldly realities will increase.

CHAPTER 6

DEVELOPING PSYCHIC SENSE-ABILITIES

The act of becoming a psychic and working in one or several Sense-Abilities is all about accessing your higher self. Your higher self is you—you in the ether. Your higher self is the real you, the more complete you; it is your total soul consciousness. It is not the you who resides here on earth. Your earth-self is only a wisp of who you really are as your higher self.

In spite of the fact that your higher self has a stronger consciousness than your earth-self, the cord existing between the two is unbreakable. Your higher self is a higher essence, with access to all your thoughts, goals, and intentions. It knows everything you think, feel, and wonder.

Our culture infuses us with a materialistic world-view that neglects the role of spirit and the existence of a higher self. If you believe in a higher self and expect benefits from communicating with that higher self, your ability to perform psychically will improve as you work to strengthen that belief and expectation. Your inner growth depends on maintaining your connection with your higher self, as does your evolving psychic Sense-Abilities.

The first priority for you in developing your psychic Sense-Abilities is to concentrate on identifying which Sense-Abilities are innate to your personality, and then focus on those. Take time to decide which skills you will explore first. These will be your first intentional adventures and experiences with the paranormal. Don't worry if you are skeptical at times. A bit of skepticism will go a long way towards making sure the psychic receptions you experience are accurately interpreted.

Skepticism, which may seem to be a deterrent to fulfilling psychic aptitude, is often beneficial in separating ordinary physical sensations, imaginings, and convoluted perceptions from actual psychic events. Skepticism is a plus, not a negative.

How we come to our lives' work is different for each person. Sometimes an interest will turn into a passion, and we dedicate ourselves to it wholeheartedly. Sometimes the path we are meant to follow is clear from the beginning, and we quietly move in that direction. In truth, we probably pursue interests in multiple ways. We may begin our lives following a conventional career and end up realizing we want more— more explanation. It is the universe speaking, urging us to turn one way or another, to travel in a new and different direction.

You may have an interest in things of the mind or in what happens after death. Both of these interests are fundamental and have, at one time or other, concerned many. However, just because you decide to pursue a path to explore these ideas, it doesn't mean you must become a psychic or medium.

Ultimately, all learning is about self-actualization and your own spiritual growth. It is all about finding out more about yourself and what you can learn. Then, if it moves you, go further down the path to become a trained psychic. If you do, you will acquire a suitable, solid foundation on which to build. Remember: the ability to access higher knowledge or to allow spirits to deliver messages to you from the other side is a skill that has to be developed. Psychic skills are a lot like muscles, which must be exercised to develop fully. The challenge is not actually being psychic, but rather believing that you are.

The goal of most psychic institutes is to help students find their way. The instructors teach students how to open the third eye (the center of all psychic ability). This opening is crucial, since it is where all psychic messages originate and where spiritual information emanates. If you question whether your third eye can be opened, question no longer. You are psychic. Every one of us is psychic. So, opening one's third eye is simple and should be effortless.

Whether we acknowledge it or not, human beings are beings of spirit. We are, on a basic and fundamental level, connected to all things that psychics tap into regularly and intentionally. Most of us spend our lives thinking and working from the left side of our brains, dealing with the sensory world, and experiencing it physically. Nevertheless, our capacities for deeper knowing are there. They are buried under piles of mundane chores and cares, concerned with everyday living. Our paths are unique and valuable. So, regardless of the extent to which we allow our intuitive/psychic knowing to develop, it can always potentially be developed.

Being a psychic isn't about seeing the future, or telling fortunes. It's about helping clients to come to their own understanding about questions causing them distress or for which they just need a bit of guidance. The issues most commonly brought to psychics—and about which psychics obtain information and messages—are requests for guidance and insight concerning health, career, finance, love, and relationships. The guidance a psychic gives is often information a client already knows but refuses to acknowledge or consider in a particular light. Often a psychic will present a client with a message or insight, and his or her response will be, "Yes, I guess I knew that."

CHAPTER 7

INTUITIVE MESSAGES AND SIGNALS

According to the Swiss psychologist Carl Jung, intuition is only one of four important functions of the human mind. It exists alongside sensations, thoughts, and emotions. Balancing these functions enables us to maximize our potential. He wrote, "I regard intuition as a basic psychological function that mediates perception in an unconscious way and enables us to divine the possibilities of a situation ..."

The more you listen to your intuition and the more you act on what you know, the more heightened your awareness will become. It is the strongest connection you will have to your subconscious mind. It is also the most important bridge between your conscious and unconscious minds. Serious seekers of supernatural connections should realize the interlinking of these two mental functions has the ability to give them unprecedented access to the source of all creativity, wisdom, and understanding. It is the link to the conceptualization of new and extraordinary thinking in the arts, music, literature, business, and science.

If you have confidence in the supernatural, you can count on being the recipient of unencumbered messages from the source of power. When you exercise psychic abilities, fortified by a strong and reinforced inner voice, you can count on the support of the universe. The only problem hindering a free flow of information is a channel contaminated by ego and self-aggrandizement. There is, however, a way to inoculate yourself against such contamination. It is self-awareness. A complete knowledge of self has the power to prevent the interference of ego and self-interest. Knowing yourself is an opportunity to fix things that prevent you from moving forward. It is also an opportunity to enhance those upright and noble parts of you. Move forward with a resolve to maintain healthy intentions and lofty goals for your psychic talents.

CHAPTER 8

THE MIND-BODY CONNECTION

Your mind isn't the only recipient of emotional signals; your body is used as a vehicle for receiving emotional messages too. The modern world keeps you focused on left-brain activities and skills. So it may take some time to become reacquainted with your emotional side. You will need to make a special effort to watch for signals emanating from your body and those generated through your thoughts. Welcome each signal by allowing it to form and then flourish.

Empathy is one of those emotional signals to which you should pay particular attention. Empathy is the intuitive gift allowing individuals to experience others' emotions as if they were their own. Healers are empathic, as are many psychics and mediums. Highly empathic individuals find they can't spend time in malls or other crowded places because of the sea of emotional responses that psychically bombards them. They're so empathic that they sense and feel the energy of everyone around them, and consequently, they become overwhelmed.

Empathy is a gift of the soul. If you are empathic, you may have to reinforce your capacity to remain balanced and centered. Grounding yourself in the here and now will enable you to find the balance you need.

People who are empathic not only connect with the feelings and energies of others, but they often feel responsible for the wellbeing of others as well. It is common for mothers to feel this way. They have a strong psychic and empathic connection to their children. However, as children grow up, mothers must learn to let go and let the children take responsibility for their lives and decisions. It can be a challenge for empathic people—particularly healers and light-workers—to let go and let others live their own lives. They have to let go without taking on their challenges or worrying about them.

If you are highly empathic, it's important to allow others to learn their own lessons and pursue their own paths. It is important to do this, regardless of any guidance you give them.

As you practice and work on opening yourself to psychic experiences, you may find you have a whole bundle of new physical and emotional experiences. Don't ignore them; keep a journal of when, where, and what you are doing or thinking when you experience a feeling. You must also begin to be more aware of your dreams. Information in dreams comes to you when it can't reach the waking mind. So develop the facility for recalling dreams. A dream journal can help make you more able to recall the higher vibrational messages delivered to you in your sleep.

Finally, it is important to drink plenty of water, get good sleep, and exercise daily. The care and attention you give to maintaining a healthy mind-body balance will serve to enhance your psychic awareness. As you take care of your body (in whatever ways work best for you), you will begin to notice a difference in your mental acuity. It is very difficult for a higher power to be housed in an unhealthy vessel. Take care of your body because it really is the temple of your soul. There is a solid relationship between a healthy body and the link with your higher power.

CHAPTER 9

THE VALUE OF MEDITATION

A number of professions readily attest to meditation as having enormous benefits for the mind and body. Professions and practices from yoga to mental health institutions to the medical community recognize meditation's ability to support efforts for maintaining a healthy mind, body, and emotional state.

Meditation is a mind-body practice that utilizes concentration, reflection, and mental relaxation. It calms the mind, rejuvenates the body, and renews the spirit. It first requires purposely clearing your mind of cluttered thinking, disconnecting from the worries and thoughts of day-to-day concerns, and then fostering moments of mental tranquility. The practice of daily meditation will result in a variety of positive effects on you and, ultimately, your training.

Different methods focus the energy of your meditations. They are all centered on managing various components of your well-being. Focused meditation provides the opportunity to hone your ability to concentrate your thoughts on a particular area. For example, meditation that concentrates on the mind encourages you to be fully present in the moment and to do away with lingering or passing thoughts that are a distraction. Focused meditation is known to increase mental alertness and efficiency.

It is easy to add a daily meditation routine to your lifestyle. It can be as simple as going for a walk and finding a calm, relatively quiet place to sit. It can be as easy as setting aside a specific time to be at peace with your thoughts, without outside distractions. Research proves that individuals who regularly practice meditation display an improvement in mental focus, self-awareness, evaluation, decision-making, and physical health.

Here is a list of specific benefits one can experience from a routine of setting time apart for reflection and meditation.

It Improves Your Communication

A calm mind and spirit allow for greater clarity of thought. A greater clarity of thought allows for greater ability to verbalize your thoughts. There is an old adage, "What is in the well of your heart comes up in the bucket of your speech." What comes up should be words to express the thoughts you intend.

It Nurtures Your Creativity

Creativity requires clear thinking and freedom from unwarranted restrictions. Relaxation and centered thought comprise the foundation of creativity. Meditation allows the mind to take in information from the universe and transform it into something useful. It provides the relaxation and freedom essential for original thinking.

It Allows You to Master Time and Glimpse Eternity

Meditation releases you from the confines of time and space. Your sense of both disappears during meditation. It also gives you the energy to work more intensely and for longer stretches, giving you laser-like focus and effectiveness. Meditation makes the time you spend on something seem shorter. It also gives you a renewed respect for quiet and leisure.

Every cell in your body is meant to exist in a state of everlasting peace, but it is your mind and limited thinking that prevent you from enjoying such an experience. Meditation changes that.

CHAPTER 10

THE DIFFERENCE BETWEEN A PSYCHIC, AN INTUITIVE, AND A MEDIUM

An psychic is one who tunes into a higher source for guidance and information. He or she connects to the universal mind and otherworldly sources to deliver guidance and information to others.

Intuitive people know things based on intellect through the use of logic, personal experiences, and learned skills; they are also extremely sensitive to what their intuition is saying. An intuitive is a master at taking information from both sources and generating effective, useful conclusions.

A medium, on the other hand, is a person with a highly developed sense of psychic awareness—someone specifically gifted with the ability to connect to the world of deceased souls. Mediums are intermediaries with the other side, and spirits work through them to bring messages to those on this earthly plane.

All psychics work on their own levels of awareness by using various Sense-Abilities to receive information to help others. For mediums, it isn't about seeing the future or telling fortunes. It's about helping people to come to their own understanding of life and its meaning through information delivered to them by departed spirits. Psychics receive messages and insights from the universal matrix on issues of health, career, finances, love, and relationships. These issues bring individuals in to see a psychic.

The guidance a psychic offers to someone often involves situations already known by the client, but for one reason or another, the answers are blocked from his or her consciousness. It is usually an issue the client refuses to acknowledge or possibly hasn't considered.

We all know more about ourselves than we think, but facing the reality of a situation may be difficult. A psychic is merely a vehicle allowing an individual to access his or her own knowledge. Psychics provide validation and give a seeker of answers the confidence needed to see a situation clearly to make his or her way forward.

If you choose to learn more about the psychic world, remember that the ability to access higher knowledge and/or allow spirits to deliver messages to you from the other side is a skill that has to be exercised. Regardless of what you attempt to learn, it is necessary to strengthen that skill and bring it from a novice level to a mastery level. You can do this with practice, diligence, and determination. The challenge for you will not be in learning the parameters of any of your Sense-Abilities or in practicing as a psychic, but in believing that psychic abilities are real—in confronting your doubt.

As you invest time and effort into growing the practice of any of the Sense-Abilities resonating with your soul-self and your intuitive aptitudes, you may notice you will become more sensitive. You will become more sensitive to the emotions emanating from your thoughts and the sensations moving through your body. Everything you experience is merely the process of becoming attuned to the vibrations, energies, and influx of information from the universe. Make sure to take note of all new sensations and experiences. They are opportunities to tap into your subconscious mind. The way you learn to connect becomes the method the universe will use to communicate with you. It will use a combination of methods unique to you.

To keep the channels between your mind and body open and receptive, it is important to treat both with respect and value. This openness will serve to enhance your overall awareness and quicken your ability to tune into the psychic world. You'll come to know when a sensation or symbol holds a message with particular meaning for you, a client, or someone close to you.

Ultimately, as we have said, all learning is about your own spiritual growth and advancement. It is about discovering more about yourself and what you want to learn. It is about moving forward on a solid foundation.

CHAPTER 11

THE VALUE OF DREAMS

Sigmund Freud called dreaming "the royal road to the unconscious." As you take on the challenge of becoming a psychic, you will learn the importance of dreams and the valuable messages they carry.

When you are working to develop Sense-Abilities, you will find it common for your dreams to change. Your dreams will take on different moods, flavors, perspectives, and importance. Colors will be more vibrant and the experiences more memorable, deeper, and more profound than ones experienced in the past. Everything in your mind and body will be changing to align with your new efforts and insights. Your energy system and its vibrational levels will be adjusting too. The avenues to the universal matrix will widen, and your ability to receive and decipher messages will increase. Connections to your higher self will strengthen, and your capacity to foster and maintain finer frequencies will become more developed. Everything will be working to elevate your skills and competencies.

Dreams have an unfathomable ability to deliver profound messages, spiritual insights, and guidance, unlike other avenues of mental access. To make the most of what you are learning, take note of every new feeling and emotion immediately after a dream; you may wish to revisit them later.

Consider, with clarity of thought, the meanings and ideas your dreams are suggesting. Dreams are an additional path leading to spiritual growth. They are proof that your perceptive abilities and powers of discernment are increasing.

Your dreams will take different forms; they may be prophetic in nature, with stronger than usual impact. Some of your dreams may involve interchanges between you and a loved one who has passed. They can act as an avenue to provide an easy, relaxed space for such encounters to occur. Each form of a dream is a message. Dreams prove there are few limitations to what we can comprehend through the psychic influences of the subconscious mind. Every opportunity to dream allows your astral body to leave the constraints of this conscious world and enter higher vibrations and dimensions—dimensions where all existence is limitless and timeless.

Why Do We Dream?

We dream because we need to. Dreams are part of our physiological and psychological makeup and are necessary to our mental and physical well-being. Humans cannot replenish their bodies or maintain their mental faculties without reaching the magical state of rapid eye movement (R.E.M.) sleep—the level that allows us to dream. Dreaming signals the proper release of chemicals and hormones our bodies need. If sleep weren't essential for us, we would have evolved beyond the need to dream long ago.

Dreams are a vehicle to help us align our emotional selves. We are able to act out unpleasant experiences, find the reasons for them, and soften their affects. Dreams also help us to problem-solve. We've all heard the phrase, "I need to sleep on it." Somehow, when our minds relax to sleep and dream, we wake with solutions we were unable to imagine without the benefit of sleep. That is why it is a good idea to keep a pen and paper by your bed, so you can record solutions before they are forgotten.

Paul McCartney came up with the words to the Beatle hit song *Yesterday* while in a dream state. Albert Einstein captured the theory of relativity while in a dream state. The inspiration behind the creation of the sewing machine came from a dream. So the dream state is a way to solve problems, as well as a schoolroom for great ideas, innovations, and inspiration.

Four Steps for Interpreting Dreams

- **Pay attention to the feelings you get in your dreams.**

  Feelings are an indication that something is important, dangerous, or worthy, and they are an emotional link to persons, places, or events in the dream. Take time to make any relevant and necessary connections; they are messages. As you become more in tune with your dream space, you will want to expand your investigation of dreams and your connection to them.

- **Trust that dreams have meaning**.

  Ask yourself, how does this dream pertain to me or have meaning to my conscious life? Trust that knowing the implications of a dream may take time. The delivery of dream messages is transcendent, and over time, the meaning will come. Those who make it a point to study their dreams often keep a dream journal they can refer to later, when an insight about a particular dream eventually presents itself. Keeping a journal ensures that every detail about a dream has been recorded, making it possible to associate those details with the essence of its possible message. That way, no point is forgotten.

- **Know that dreams have applications to the past, present, and future.**

  Dream messages aren't always about what is currently happening in your life or the lives of those you know. They can bring messages that warn of past behaviors, give meaning to past events, or point out the importance of past activities. They can also be prophetic in nature. Much can be learned through information made available by dreams; it should not be ignored.

- **Look for the relevancy of a dream.**

  Question the information in your dreams, and search out what is most useful and valuable. Question whether any connection can be made to other events in your life or the lives of others. Dreams are not just random thoughts or ruminations. They are transmissions from the universal matrix. Important things happening in your waking life can instigate a dream. Matters in your waking life are often crying out for answers and explanations. Dreams often have those answers.

Dream Tips

- Tune into the feelings of your dream, and other insights will come.
- Give your dreams the level of importance they deserve.
- Create your own dream dictionary or book of symbols.
- Remember: you are the best person to interpret your dreams.
- Trust that dreams serve to enrich your life.

Remember: your dreams are a valuable and rich source of guidance and information. The depth of your spiritual connection to all that exists in this world and the world beyond is expanded through dreaming.

Dream Interpretation and a Book of Symbols

The best person to interpret your dreams is you. Years ago, people would consult a dream encyclopedia, manual, or dictionary in which everything that could happen in a dream was cataloged, along with a corresponding interpretation. While the attempt at this type of dream interpretation was honest, the application was so general that it was impractical and irrelevant to the seeker. The best way to get a handle on knowing whether incidences—recurring or not—have a particular meaning is to create a book of symbols pertinent to only you.

First, make it a point to have a journal or notepad nearby before you go to bed. Second, pay close attention to any images that stand out in your dream, and immediately, upon waking, jot them down. Pay attention to colors, sounds, the setting, objects such as a car, house, or water, and even other people. Most importantly, be mindful of any emotions that present in your dream. Often it is the last dream before you awaken that will be the most meaningful for you. Lastly, connect any of those images, happenings, or ideas to your waking life that appear to be strongly associated. These associations will be apparent each time a dream experience occurs. Your book of symbols will be an accumulation of documented information and will serve as your reference for interpretations.

Tips to Quiet Your Mind

A quiet mind and a sense of inner peace are essential for an effective and insightful psychic. They are necessary for anyone to whom creativity, discernment, perception, and clear thinking are important. A quiet mind is perhaps the first and most valuable quality an aspiring psychic should acquire.

1. Take time to do nothing. Find a quiet place that speaks to your soul, and spend time in that space as often as you can.

2. Meditate. It slows thinking, slows breathing, and slows worldly awareness. It actually shifts your brain. It temporarily adjusts the parts of your brain called the lateral prefrontal cortex and the medial prefrontal cortex. The lateral prefrontal cortex is responsible for modulating your emotional responses and automatic behaviors and habits. The medial prefrontal cortex is responsible for constantly reviewing past experiences, responses, and behaviors. These two automatic sets of responses work to prevent you from quieting your mind. Meditation slows those responses and gives you enough control to allow you to truly quiet your mind.

3. Acknowledge any feelings of being rushed, feelings of anguish, or feelings of tension. Acknowledge your willingness to give into compulsive habits (smoking, drinking, TV watching, overeating). Acknowledge that those feelings exist, and then simply stop and take three breaths. This action instantly breaks your connection with compulsion and generates an awareness of your surroundings instead. A subtle feeling of peaceful energy will pervade your body and thereby lay a foundation for future peace.

4. Pay attention to the energy fields operating inside your body. See compulsive energies as separate and apart from you, and then use the power of thought to employ conscious breathing.

5. Pay attention to how you are breathing, and make a conscious effort to breathe slowly and rhythmically. You will soon feel negative emotions and compulsive urges disappear. As awareness of your emotions grows and as you deliberately halt incessant thinking, you will begin to exercise control of those emotions, giving you space for quiet contemplation and peace.

Most people are so distracted by their thoughts they can no longer feel the infusion of life that breathing brings. Whenever you can, when it comes to mind, center on your breath. This practice is more spiritually transformative than any book, course, coaching, or lesson of any kind.

CHAPTER 12

PSYCHIC SENSE-ABILITIES (CLAIR ABILITIES)

All Sense-Abilities are avenues by which to see the world as it really is. Psychic abilities without a purposeful intention to do good for others are skills that can be learned and, as such, are merely skills. Skills are just that—skills. Psychic awareness, psychic abilities, psychic creativity, and spiritual growth present opportunities for supernatural practices to serve personal growth and the needs of humankind. When psychic potential is unleashed, and you can see what it manifests, you know that it is probably worth your while to pursue it.

But first things first. Decide the focus your psychic ability will take. Connecting with your higher self, your sixth sense, and the spirit world requires the use of all your senses: taste, touch, smell, hearing, and sight. These senses are the doorways through which your connection with your intuitive, psychic self develops. Through your Sense-Abilities, you take your physical senses to a higher spiritual level. This process becomes a *heightened sensing*. Psychic Sense-Abilities come in many forms, and the development of any psychic ability takes time and energy.

The first thing to do before attempting to invest in any kind of formal training is to get a sense of your own inner Sense-Abilities.

Start by taking time to increase awareness of everything around you. Try taking a sensory field trip—a time when all you do is practice awareness. Go to a zoo, the woods, your local grocery store, or farmer's market. Take time to notice everything there. Take thirty to forty minutes to wander around. Listen to the sounds that make up the environment, the smells you encounter, and everything you rarely take notice of. Look everywhere, and feel everything. Feel textures, notice colors, sensations, temperatures, and smells. Handle things. Notice the weight and temperature of the items you touch.

What is happening all around you? Is it colder or warmer in certain parts of the store? What are you feeling on the inside of your body? What are you feeling on the outside of your body? Are you drawn to look up, down, or to the side for any reason? If so, ask yourself why. It is important to notice direction because of the way things present; looking from top to bottom, from right or left matters.

Take into account how you are feeling along the way; attempt to ascertain what reactions you are having and why. Keep track of what keeps you from focusing and what may be the cure. Focus on the smallest details; write down every experience as you go, but don't allow your writing to distract you. Jot down just a word or two to remind you of each experience. You can focus on the writing later.

Noticing directions is important, as directional messages are correlated with time. For example, something presenting from the left can mean it is linked to the past, from the middle, a link to the present, and from the right, a future connection.

The sensory field trip will help you access which Sense-Abilities you are predisposed to practice. You will get a sense of what your innate talents are. Each of the Sense-Abilities is a complementary tool, available to psychics through the way they access information— information which can't be learned any other way.

It is possible you will find what particular affinity you have for one or several Sense-Abilities. You will find those Sense-Abilities form the foundation for your activities with clients. You will also find that each Sense-Ability grows in development and intensity. Be aware of what kind of information is most likely to be revealed to you and through which Sense-Ability it is most likely to come. Remember not to dismiss anything that is unfamiliar or strange. Be bold and open to what was previously closed to you.

Once you have determined which sense is the strongest for you, sit in a comfortable, quiet position. Become aware of your body and your breathing. Breathe in and out slowly for a minute or so. Then, give attention to the Sense-Ability with which you connect the strongest. Next, simultaneously be mindful of your breath and your Sense-Ability, as if they were one. If hearing is the most prominent of your senses, then focus your attention on your ears. Breathe in and out slowly, focusing for several minutes on the fact that you and your ears are one. If your Sense-Ability is Taste Reception, focus on your tongue, and exhale and inhale as you do so. Each day, when it comes to your attention, take time to repeat this exercise with your dominant Sense-Ability in mind. Concentration will make your particular Sense-Ability more firmly instilled in your mind.

Become comfortable with your hunches and Receptive Discernment. Learn to trust them. If something doesn't feel right, chances are it isn't. What may be right for one person may be totally wrong for another. We have all experienced times when a feeling deep in the stomach compels us to take action. If we don't listen to this prompting, we might feel as though we had missed doing something central to our benefit or the benefit of someone else. There are times when we've listened to such an urging, only to learn that listening made a difference and was important.

Your sixth-sense is your inner guide. Learn to trust it. It may be scary at first, and it may appear to lack logical sense, but you will soon discover it does make sense. When you obey your urges and listen to your inner-self, you'll reinforce the power of your awareness and see it become an important part of how your life (and the lives of others) obtains a deeper understanding of certain events.

Pay attention and be aware. The more data and information you absorb, the more your subconscious mind will reveal. Your intuitive senses use all the information gathered from your conscious mind. They allow your subconscious mind to play a part in delivering information to aid in your decision-making. Remember: your subconscious mind communicates information directly to your conscious mind, and it does so through the power of your inner perceptions. It is important for the development of your psychic abilities to pay attention to even the smallest hints and clues you receive. The key to a fully integrated experience is to take notice.

If you have ever ignored your intuition or inner observations and later had to deal with unpleasant consequences, you know the importance of paying attention. Remember: the more you pay attention, the more you will experience. The more you experience, the clearer and more correct your messages will be.

Use the power of sleep. Much can be learned and explored while your consciousness visits the unconscious realm. Put your subconscious mind to work while you sleep. Before you go to bed at night, reflect on any questions or issues for which you need solutions. Your subconscious mind will consider the problem and make an answer apparent to you in the morning. Since dreams and sleep information are often lost in the presence of the conscious mind—the light of day—have a pen and book light available for recording what you have discovered.

Journaling will also help. When you take time to record your experiences, you give yourself the ability to evaluate and appraise the whys and wherefores of your experiences. It is an excellent way to give meaning to inner messages, insights, and unexpected knowledge. Remember: the development of your personal awareness is akin to learning a new skill. The more you practice, the better you will become.

CHAPTER 13

A LOOK AT THE SENSE-ABILITIES (CLAIRS)

Visual Reception (Clairvoyance) is one of the six major intuitive abilities. It is the ability with which most people are familiar. It is also the one with the greatest public recognition and largest reputation for exhibiting the most dramatic, supernatural results and influence. In spite of their popularity, however, all Sense-Abilities are just as impactful and just as dramatic. Each Sense-Ability has a specific place in the realm of psychic predilections; Visual Reception is only one among many.

Visual Reception, in its purest form, is the ability—using vision—to obtain a higher vibrational frequency in the world of the paranormal. A Visual Receptive can see a symbol, number, color, or image of any kind. But the message may be so subtle that he or she is not aware of its meaning. On the other hand, the Visual Receptive may have a full-blown premonition, with the message and the meaning being clear and concise.

Visual Receptives have the ability to gaze into the spiritual realm through their minds' eyes and detect such things as nonphysical energies. Those with this ability receive extrasensory impressions, symbols, and meanings in the form of mental images, attained without the aid of physical vision. These receptions enable them to see beyond the confines of time, space, and location of events and messages from the past, present, or future.

This Sense-Ability is often referred to as the third eye, an invisible, inner eye, which is the gateway to visual perception transcending ordinary sight. If you have ever had a daydream, then you have experienced what it's like to use your inner eye or Visual Reception. It really is that simple.

Try it now. Take a moment, look around you, and pick an item. Now close your eyes, and see that item in your mind's eye. Look at the details of it— the color, the shades of color, and the texture. Are there particular shapes and sizes? As you do this, you are recalling visually but in a new and heightened way. This simple visualization is how it will feel to see images, so remember this feeling. Images come naturally, gently, and in their own time

As you work on this ability, you might try using a reading screen as a place for images to present. You can think of a reading screen like a viewing receptacle. Using your mind's eye, imagine a large chalk board or computer monitor in front of you. Ask a question. Don't demand; just ask. Relax, and be the observer as the answer comes to the reading screen. Trust, expect, and intend that your ability is there. Just set the intention to let your Visual Reception ability open.

The first image that comes will be your answer, be it symbolic or literal. Make note of symbols, colors, shapes, letters, and numbers, and be open to whatever comes. Your desire to understand fully the meaning of the images or to make images come is rooted in ego. Release this desire. Images may be brief at first, much like bursts. This is okay. You also may find yourself unsure about the meaning of what you are seeing. This too is normal. Meaning and interpretation will come as this ability grows.

Emotional Reception (Clairsentience) is the ability to receive intuitive messages via feelings, emotions, or physical sensations. It is having a sense of what is going on inside another person's life, emotional state, personal relationships, fears, and challenges.

Those with this ability are Emotional Receptives. They tune into psychic messages without anyone's help or the help of their five senses. Emotional Receptives feel the physical and emotional conditions of others, whether those conditions are in the present, in the past, or in the future. They receive sensations from locales, buildings, houses, and other physical objects. They are also proficient at detecting and sensing an individual's aura.

Emotional Receptives are empathetic individuals. They not only sense things, but they literally feel them within their bodies. They may feel vibrations or the resonance of an emotion—a sympathetic exchange between the Emotional Receptive's body and the body of someone else. Such an exchange is common in psychic healing. The emotional or physical sensation experienced by an Emotional Receptive can be as clear as an image coming through Visual Reception (something seen) or through smells experienced by those capable of Scent Reception.

Emotional Reception is about emotion and empathy. If you are deeply in touch with your own emotions and are able to share in the emotions of others easily, you are probably an Emotional Receptive. For example, extrasensory stimuli may send a chill down your spine, make the hair on your arm stand up, or give you a sick feeling in your stomach. Psychics gifted with Emotional Reception are able to retrieve information from feelings, public buildings, and outdoor environments.

If you have the gift of an Emotional Receptive, you may experience a strong emotional feeling or physical sensation about a place or about an individual during a first meeting. Many individuals who have this ability often do not consciously realize it. They only know they don't feel right about things. They may enter a public space and immediately feel overwhelmed, sad, anxious or elated—experiences that may consume them and make it difficult to differentiate which feelings belong to them and which belong to someone in close proximity. They may also get small glimpses of events that have taken place or will take place.

Professionally trained psychics learn to take emotional messages seriously, and rather than ignore or dismiss them, they zero in on the meaning. They focus on their emotional and physical reactions in an effort to learn what message is being sent and what lesson is to be learned. To those in whom these feelings are common, it is an opportunity to gain valuable insights to help others.

The gift of Emotional Reception also includes receiving emotions through physical means. Many in the psychic field consider Emotional Reception as a highly evolved form of empathy. They are sensitive to the energies that surround people, places, and things and are capable of receiving information by touching an object. Such information is the transmission of an emotion through a physical object. The experience is something like an electrical current or a nervous response.

This intake of physical information can overpower an individual. Emotional Receptives are so sensitive to the energies surrounding them that they often find themselves besieged by emotions too difficult to manage. An Emotional Receptive or empath must learn to manage the input of emotions and the physical reactions that accompany them. They must put these emotional connections into a space where they can acknowledge them and their physical manifestations as just information to be communicated and nothing more. This takes practice, but people so endowed are mandated to submit to their gifts and deliver the messages they receive.

If Emotional Reception is an ability you have identified for your yourself, you may say things like, "The way I *feel* when you talk is …" as opposed to "What I *hear* you saying is …"

If you often use the word *feel*, then you are probably an Emotional Receptive (clairsentient). If you express yourself using the word *hear*, then you are most likely an Audible Receptive (clairaudient). If you find yourself feeling the emotions of others or walking into a room and sensing the energy of the people in it, then you are an Emotional Receptive.

If you give attention to the feelings of your daily experiences, then you are an Emotional Receptive. So, as you work through the issues of importance in your life, it is most likely that you consider your emotions or the emotions of others before anything else. You probably recall emotional connections, impressions, and feelings when recounting your dreams.

While it is common to have two or more of the Sense-Abilities, you will have to determine which of them is the strongest or whether you are endowed equally with all of them. As you grow in your knowledge of psychic abilities, you become better at identifying your psychic strengths, and you learn more about how you interact psychically with the world around you. You will learn that the gateway to Emotional Reception is located in your second chakra. Your second chakra is bright orange and spins in a clockwise direction. It will help you focus, relax, and open up to the part of you that is sensitive to your psychic ability.

Audible Reception (Clairaudience) is the ability to decipher and receive messages sent from the universal matrix by way of sounds, words, and extrasensory noises. These sounds can be heard through one's inner ear and are unheard by others. They are sounds occurring beyond the parameters of the natural world. They can be voices, unidentifiable sounds, or music inaudible by normal hearing.

Audible Receptives hear sounds mentally or in their heads. They are actually receiving information in the form of voices or noises significant to the reading at hand. It is hearing on a higher level and similar to reading silently and hearing the words in your mind. It is as though you are replaying words of a previous conversation. Sometimes the sounds are more like vibrations, subtle and gentle, which can signal the coming and going of spirits. They are a sign that psychic connections are established and a free flow of information is happening.

Sometimes the messages are the sounds of someone repeating prior conversations or phrases from the past. Oftentimes, the sounds are physically audible, but only the Audible Receptive can make sense of it. The information the spirits deliver in this way is related to current happenings, but they can also relate to the past or the future. Messages can also be warnings to avoid a course of action about a career, a move, or another important decision.

Audible Reception messages can come from your higher self and from your spiritual collective. Since spirits communicate telepathically, their messages are heard internally. To begin an experience with Audible Reception, take a moment to focus on the layers of sounds around you just before you go to bed at night. There is a symphony of sounds happening, if you attempt to recognize them. Give your attention to all the sounds and noises you hear in the distance. Be with the sounds for a few moments. Next, listen to any humming or sounds close by. Now, go within yourself and listen to your breath and the sounds within you. Do you hear someone's voice in your head? Whose voice is it? Is it yours?

Finally, listen to sounds that are deeper than your breath. Listen to the sounds hidden in the silence. There is a symphony there too. Is it whining? Buzzing? Whirring? Vibrating? Imagine what it may sound like to hear a grain of sand fall. Can you hear the humming of the stars? Listen to the sounds that occur in the void of nothingness.

Meditation has the ability to open you up to audible channels that will help in your psychic work. The key is not to be afraid of what you may hear, understanding that it simply involves a desire from the spirits to communicate.

Examples of Audible Reception:

- You hear your name being called from a disembodied voice.

- You overhear a conversation in which a stranger talks about something you need desperately to hear—an answer, a warning.
- You hear the voice of a loved one calling to you for help, but that loved one is too far away for you to hear. Upon investigation, you find you were needed at the moment you heard the call.
- A voice gives you a life-changing message.
- You hear a strong message to follow a particular direction, deliver a message, or perform a particular task.
- You hear a knock on the door no one else hears; upon opening it, you find someone is breaking into your car.
- You hear a shrill ringing in your ear that compels you to stop what you are doing.

Receptive Discernment (Claircognizance) is an awareness of information, without the benefit of previous knowledge or facts. Receptive Discernment, unlike other psychic aptitudes, comes without a corresponding physical response. It is strictly the calm assurance and strong emotion of something the Discerner knows he or she cannot prove. However, time and circumstance often reveal the truth of his or her statements. Receptive Discernment can be powerful and impactful because it requires no interpretation.

This is one of the psychic aptitudes most often dismissed because it comes without warning or recognizable reason. It appears to come out of the blue, without a realization of where the information came from or how to defend its authenticity. While everyone has experienced this inflow of information, few believe it to be reliable. When strengthened, this ability will happen more often and more strongly. Consequently, the Discerner's information will be seen as more credible.

It's important to trust yourself when receiving any form of inner guidance and to evaluate the information in terms of how often it comes to you and how often it has been right. You will be giving credibility to your inner perceptions and discernment. The mind sometimes taps into things that can't be known through ordinary physical means. When this happens, people say such things as, "I don't know; it just felt right." Or, "It just didn't feel right to go in there."

This kind of psychic knowledge may be a residual from our evolutionary past, when we were defenseless animals in need of extra protection. Allowing us to survive as a species are our powers of the mind and our ability to trust our feelings—feelings we now commonly refer to as our *inner voice*. Receptive Discernment is different than everyday thoughts, feelings, or notions, and as your psychic ability matures, you will be able to tell the difference between a regular thought and Receptive Discernment (knowing).

Receptive Discernment presents itself as inspired ideas, dreams, or automatic writing and often presents during meditation or while giving or receiving a psychic reading. The information may appear to be a gut feeling or a sense that you know something but aren't sure how you know it. Messages may also be received unconsciously. They may come in the form of creativity. These feelings or emotions will correctly guide you if you pay attention. Your emotions are the best compass to discern credible information.

To enhance Receptive Discernment, focus on seeing yourself as separate from any message that comes in. Resist the temptation to interpret; just look from the outside in. Be an observer. Messages emanating from your ability to Receptively Discern may seem to come from nowhere, may seem spontaneous, and most often, have little to do with what you are thinking at any given moment.

Receptive Discernment information and insights are of a high vibrational frequency and transcend ego. If you notice low vibrational thoughts of fear, worry, doubt, or self-sabotage when you tune into this ability, you are failing to connect to your gift of Discernment. It may take time to understand Receptive Discernment messages, but that is okay. The knowing will come when it is ready to do so.

A Tool for Developing Receptive Discernment: Automatic Writing

A helpful tool that will assist you in developing this Sense-Ability is automatic writing.

- Take a moment to formulate a question you desire to know an answer to.
- Say the question out loud.
- As the observer, start writing. Write down what comes naturally and easily. It may be words or sketches or even what seem like mere scribbles. It may come in a picture you are inspired to draw. Let the information come, and write it down. Remember: you are an observer to all the information presented.
- Repeat this three times on three separate sheets of paper, giving yourself about two to three minutes for each writing.
- Set the writing aside, and return to it later to evaluate and interpret what you have written and where your answer is in the writing. If you have drawn images, be sure to turn your paper to view the images from different perspectives.

Scent Reception (Clairalience): The spirit world and the universal matrix send messages in a myriad of ways. One of those ways enlists the power of aromas, odors, and smells not available in the environment. They are smells and odors intended to send a message to the Scent Receptive for a reason important to those around the Receptive or to alert him or her of the presence of spirits.

It is not unusual for Scent Receptives to encounter a particular scent connected with the spirit of a loved one who has passed on. It is possible for the scent to be the aroma of perfume the person wore, a favorite food the person cooked, or the tobacco the person smoked. It is an indication that the spirit is present and may have a message to convey. Many people encounter familiar scents when their loved ones are visiting in spirit. Scent Reception is often a gentle precursor to seeing and interacting with visiting spirits.

Taste Reception (Clairgustance): This is probably the most unusual of all psychic phenomena. It is a form of extrasensory perception allowing the gifted person to taste a substance associated with someone or something from the past, present, or future. Psychics with this ability experience a variety of taste sensations, without actually placing anything on their tongues or into their mouths.

Taste Reception enables the Receptive to receive messages from the spiritual realm by experiencing the essence of a particular flavor, as if it were an actual physical flavor. The benefit here is to be able to taste things essential to a spiritual message, without the risk of being harmed.

Taste Reception, like Scent Reception, is closely linked to delivering messages from the spirits of those who have departed. It enables the Taste Receptive to communicate accurately the descriptions of the loved one by relating their favorite food or cooking habits. Imagine a Taste Receptive being able to relate the essence of a grandmother's casserole or a deceased father's custom of using too much salt.

The gift of taste is not only applicable to receiving messages from someone who is deceased (or to some nonphysical entity), but it can also be linked to the living. The Taste Receptive may experience taste sensations associated with people they know. A visit from a friend obsessed with sweets may be signaled by the taste of candy each time the friend is about to visit.

Let's experience the power of this ability. Take a moment to imagine a lemon. Visualize it in all its vibrant, yellow color. What shape is it? Is the lemon cold or warm? If you could touch it, what would the texture feel like? Take a gentle whiff of the air as if you were smelling the lemon. Now, imagine the lemon being cut into two pieces, and watch as the tart juices escape. Next, as if the lemon were right out in front of you, stick out your tongue, and lick the juicy, sour center of the lemon. Notice the tastes and sensations in your mouth. Do you taste the sour of the lemon? What is happening with your tongue? For many of you, saliva may be creating in your mouth as you are doing this visualization. In this moment, you taste the lemon in a heightened way.

It is important to note that Taste Reception is seldom experienced alone, without the accompaniment of Scent Reception. These two abilities work side by side and enhance each other. All the other Sense-Abilities, like Visual Reception, benefit from these two Sense-Abilities. For the psychic, the ability to see or hear something psychically is enhanced when smells and taste are a part of the experience.

The above Sense-Abilities all involve receiving messages from the universal mind and spirits located in the spiritual realm. They involve receiving signs for the express purpose of delivering information. Receiving these messages isn't complicated; anyone can be a courier, if they choose to be.

Other Important Receptions

Spirit Interactors (Mediumship): Spirit Interactors use their power to detect and communicate with spirits and those in the afterlife for the purpose of conveying specifically targeted information to a specific, living individual.

Spirit Interactors serve as live, human interactors for spirits existing on the astral plane. Interactors serve as Receptives for multiple types of energy emanating from the spirit world and/or the universal matrix. An Interactor seeks out spirits on behalf of the living, and spirits seek out cooperative Interactors for delivering information to the living. Spirits also seek out Interactors in order to be revealed, become materialized, or influence a course of events.

Where spirit connections are concerned, several well-defined types of phenomena occur. Communication is one, but another is the manipulation of energy systems. There are, therefore, two types of spirit connections/interactions: mental and physical. Mental connections involve mental telepathy—the transfer of information through thought, with the assistance of one's physical senses. The Interactor may receive the information through objects he or she mentally sees, hears, and/or feels. While the information comes across and is delivered as words, the actual transmission of the information comes in the form of a thought.

With a Spirit-Interaction reading, the images and messages received will be an evidential reference to something significant about the person for whom you are conducting the reading or regarding the spirit presenting. Actual names, dates, and events often present in this kind of session, to the extent it is known that a loved one is present.

In a psychic reading, clues and messages come through symbols with a more general meaning. For example, when you see an image of a heart, you may assume a love relationship is involved. If that heart is torn in two, it may mean there is something troublesome about the relationship—a breakup or separation. Such symbolic messages are more prevalent in a psychic session, yet in a Spirit-Interaction reading, spirits tend to converse in factual, evidential information.

When you experience validation by a spirit while in a reading, it is enormously powerful to all who witness it. When a spirit comes through in a medium session, it is profound. It not only provides validation of your ability to connect to the other side, but it is an indication that the work of Spirit Interactions is for you.

It is important to note that individuals' transitions to the other side can be new to them. At the same time you're processing your grief at their loss, they are transitioning from this world to a new world and a new space. Prayers help them find their way. It is possible for you to create a kind of soft landing for them, which they will consider helpful.

It is also important to realize that the other side is not a place like heaven or hell—a place traditionally described by traditional religions. The other side exists on the astral plane, a place of energy instead of physical matter, similar to what we experience in our world. The concept of an astral plane is common in other cultures and has been around in Western thought since before the Romans. Energy on the astral plane vibrates at a much higher frequency than it does here on the earthly plane. The most common sensation reported by the spirits is that it is one of beautiful calm and peaceful communion among spirits. In our physical existence, the most common experience is one of conflict and desire. The complete dissolution of troubling and hostile sensations on the astral is, in itself, unique.

Although the astral plane is a place of peace for the departed, that experience is not given to those conducting Spirit Interactions. Any experience with the afterlife requires a debriefing and a psychic cleansing. It is necessary in order to perform this work safely and effectively.

Physical Interactions with spirits involve such things as the familiar table interactions you've seen in movies—trances—with or without the takeover of the Interactor's voice. They often involve the manipulation or changes of the physical environment, its systems, or its energies. Physical Spirit Interaction is rare, but because of the interest and appeal to the curious, it may lead to false expectations by those seeking to communicate with spirits. So it is important for those who wish to become involved with psychic phenomenon and spirit communications to protect themselves against negative energy and psychic attacks.

Caution: psychic attacks occur when dark, negative energy vibrations are sent from one individual to another, or there is a disturbance in the energetic and physical fields of a person's body or environment. It is also possible to be misused by the spirits you encounter or with which you communicate. If you endeavor to enter into any psychic work, the work of Spirit Interaction, or the relaxed interaction with clients, it behooves you to take precautions to protect yourself. Your mind and body are great receptors for emotional stimuli and negative feelings. Take note, such occurrences may not originate from within you; they may be emanating from without. As you become more in tune with your energy, you may become more sensitive to energy of all kinds.

Your pure, positive essence should be the only energy allowed in your space. So, establish the routine of a prayer of protection, and place a protection rose around your aura to assist you in your day to day activities, your meditations, or any kind of spiritual work. Do this in order to keep yourself surrounded by healthy energies. Remember: you are spirit, and your spirit has space. It's important to maintain an awareness of your own sacred space.

A protection rose is a boundary—an invisible space you create and place at the edge of your aura. It acts as a filter or receptacle to absorb energies around you that are not your own and do not belong in your space. It helps you become aware of the boundary between where your energy ends and the rest of world begins. A protection rose can also serve as a wakeup call—to be mindful of your need of protection. For example, when the thought of protection occurs, it is a clue to be aware. Center yourself by making a conscientious effort to be present in the moment and undistracted by mind noise. Tune in to the events and occurrences around you. The protection rose is a signal to be mindful of healthy energy, your boundaries, and the energy that may be flowing inward and outward.

Protecting yourself is extremely important when working with clients. After you complete a session, it's important to release energy that may have built up during a connection. Sit quietly and meditate. Work to recall your energy that may have dissipated or remained with those from the other side. Release the energies you received from the spirits or from your client, and send them from your space. You may not be aware of it, but spiritual residue can build up like the sludge in an automobile engine and can cause mental and emotional disturbances down the road.

In addition to mentally incorporating a protection rose, it may help to imagine cords of outside energy, connecting to your energy, which you can disconnect with an imaginary pair of scissors. Not releasing these cords can drain your body and create confusion in your space. These cords usually attach themselves to your chakra points, alerting you to become aware of which ones affect you the most. Ask your spirit guides to clear them for you at the end of a reading. A psychic cleansing is not only advisable but also necessary to remain clear and in control of your own power. When you take your training, you will learn different methods of cleansing. For now, just know that such a ritual is important for keeping yourself safe and clear.

So, if you are feeling unusually out of sorts, suffering unusual dreams, experiencing pains or other physical symptoms without reason or consistency, you may be experiencing residual low vibration energy which just needs to be released.

CHAPTER 14

MESSAGES FROM LOVED ONES

You don't have to be a medium to receive messages from a spirit or a loved one who has passed over to the other side. Signs and symbols from our loved ones happen regularly and in a number of different ways. Once you open the door to those signs and symbols, you will realize they are not just coincidental happenings. Messages come from loved ones in the following ways:

Electricity

One of the easiest ways spirit come to us is through electricity. Electricity acts as a conductor for spirits. When lights flicker, computers and televisions randomly shut off and on, light bulbs burst, telephones die, and other physical phenomenon occur for no apparent reason, take notice. It may be a spirit attempting to communicate. Stop and take a moment to ask yourself which of your loved ones might be trying to reach you.

Dreams

Dreams are one of the best ways to connect with and receive messages from spirits. If you desire to connect with loved ones, simply ask them to come and visit you before you go to bed at night. Then, expect they will come. Don't try too hard; trust they have heard you and will approach when they are ready. Pay attention to the colors, symbols, words, and people in your dreams. You will know your loved one is communicating because the dream will be more vivid than usual.

Feeling Your Loved One

You may simply feel the presence of a loved one. You may experience a warm feeling or a strong sense that your loved one is nearby. You may feel a chill or a light touch on your shoulder that forces you to turn, finding no one there. It is quite possible that this touch is just one of the ways a spirit is signaling its presence.

Smell

Smell is a strong and powerful way a spirit may choose to communicate. You may experience the smell of a great aunt's cologne or a grandfather's pipe tobacco. You may even smell odors of shared times and events. These smells may present themselves at the oddest times, signaling the presence of a spirit that wants to be noticed.

Thinking of Them

Recalling or thinking about a departed loved one is an excellent indication that a spirit is communicating with you. This is especially true if the thoughts are strong and happen at an unusual time or in an unusual place. It is quite likely that a loved one is thinking of you at that very moment or coming to let you know he or she is nearby. Our loved ones on the other side know exactly what they are doing, and they have the ability to be at the right place at the right time.

Coincidence and Synchronistic Events

We are often presented with what might be called a unique, synchronistic event. Be aware of the message. There really is no such thing as coincidence. If you have ever thought of a loved one, are then reminded of favorite song you shared, and later that day, heard it on the radio, it may be the interface of a loved one.

Numbers

Do you see numbers that seem to repeat themselves? Do clocks stop at a certain time? Do license plate numbers have a particularly important sequence? Do you see a loved one's birth date routinely showing up? It may be the obvious nudge of an important spirit.

The ways in which our loved ones communicate are as varied and complicated as their personalities. There is no one way for that communication to happen. It can be any one or all of those mentioned above. No matter what means is used to get through to you, it is important not to discount the happening. Be mindful of so-called coincidences. Listen, and open yourself to their needs and ways to interact with you.

CHAPTER 15

INITIATING SPIRIT COMMUNICATION

Interactors are often the ones who initiate Spirit Interactions, but spirits may be the ones to initiate a contact as well. However, it is possible for you to initiate a connection on your own in spite of the fact that you lack training. Here are ways to go about it.

Ask

Spirits will come when invited. They honor your space, and they don't just drop in without permission. You may want to request they show you a symbol or sign when they are ready to come through. This will give you a clear indication that you have been heard, and the spirit is ready to respond.

Be Open

We often carry certain desires and expectations about connecting with a particular loved one. Try to let go of any preconceived notions of how such an experience should go, and most importantly, believe in the spirit's ability to reach you. It will come in many forms—some unexpected.

Be Patient

Your loved ones are on schedules of their own and are adjusting to being on the other side in much the same way you are adjusting to their passing. Think of it as if they are getting situated in a new home. Give them time to settle. It will help them make the transition easier.

Simply tell your loved ones that you are perfectly willing to receive their messages when they are ready to communicate. Also, remember that wanting to communicate too eagerly may hinder communication. Be decisive, objective, and confident, so the spirit can feel comfortable enough to trust you. Be free of expectations, and the event will come to fruition in a way that is natural and free-flowing.

State your Intention

State aloud your intention to open the door through which to speak and receive messages from the spirit world. Whether you encounter interaction on a personal level or in a formal reading session, know that the universe hears you. There is a divine plan in place greater than you and your intention. Allow things to happen.

Tune In

In your daily meditation, be sure to quiet your logical, left brain thinking. Say hello and then goodbye to your left brain. Make an agreement with your left brain to reconvene at another time. Meditation and a quiet mind will assist in a quicker and clearer connection with a spirit.

Be Aware

The next important step in your journey is watching for signs, symbols, and messages during your day. Links to the spirit world may come in dreams, songs, and in synchronistic-like events, which you assume are coincidences. But, coincidence is nonexistent. Everything is intentional and has a place. Everything is meant to happen.

Use Your Sense-Abilities

Connecting with the spirit world requires the use of all of your senses: taste, touch, smell, hearing, feeling, and seeing. Therefore, the practice of any one of the Sense-Abilities takes your physical senses to a higher spiritual level. It is the practice of one or more of the Sense-Abilities that gives deeper meaning to the function of your senses.

A Technique for Sensing Spirit Energies

Another way to train yourself to be aware of the energies of a spirit is to choose two people (one living and one deceased) whom you know well. Obtain a picture of the people you have chosen. It's important that you are familiar with the people you have chosen, because you will also be familiar with their energy. It is much easier to learn how to sense energy when you know the persons and have had a relationship with them. Next, have a notebook and pen to record what you experience.

Here are the steps for one type of an energy detection technique:

1. Sit in a relaxed position. Place your nondominant hand over the photo of the living person, palm facing upward in an attitude of receptivity. Now give some thought to the person. Remember to be mindful of your breath. You don't have to look at the photo, but rather, feel the thoughts of the person as the thoughts

begin to emanate. Record what memories come to mind, what feelings you sense inside and outside of your body. Can you see what that person is wearing? Do you hear the voice? What is the person saying? Is there a smell present? Or, are you aware of a color? Write everything down that presents itself to you. Information is connected to the spirit's energy. There is no right or wrong in this process.

2. When you are ready, go through the same process with the second photograph—the photograph of the deceased person. Again, give an easy and gentle thought to him or her, and just allow yourself to be a receptacle for receiving whatever comes. Sense the energy of the picture, and visualize the individual. Take notes of all that is presented. Take notes about what you learn about them, and most importantly, tune into his or her energy. Release any desire to fixate on any particular thing or memory. Just breathe, and gently focus on sensing the energy there.

3. Now take time to write down the unique differences between the energy and feeling of the deceased person versus the living person. The feeling may be slight, but trust that your subconscious self has fully grasped this difference. Your conscious self may not be so attentive and may need more time and practice in order to become aware.

Practicing this technique is a valuable gateway for opening yourself to spirit energies. Repeat this exercise several times. When you become more adept, try adding photographs of people you don't know, living and deceased. Consider well-known leaders, athletes, and other influential people. The energy of such people is unique, strong, and easier to discern. In time, and with consistent practice, you will be able to clearly distinguish a concrete feel for each energy type.

CHAPTER 16

DISTANT SENSING (CONTROLLED REMOTE VIEWING)

Distant Sensing (also called Controlled Remote Viewing or CRV) is an advanced psychic skill enabling a practitioner to mentally see objects hundreds or even thousands of miles away. It is an activity whereby a psychic practitioner tunes in to an object, location, or event inaccessible by normal means—regardless of time, distance, or location.

Distant Sensing is implemented when an individual requests a psychic practitioner (a Distant Sensor) to look into a past event or request a visit to a location as it existed in the past. It is also used when someone wants to view or peek at something locked or hidden away. Once the Distant Sensor locates the object or event and views it, the Distant Sensor will report the revealed information to the individual. The Distant Sensor does this by using a structured process, incorporating written information, verbal statements, or illustrated sketches.

Distant Sensors are often asked to *see* places or objects situated in unreachable locations, which may be on the other side of the globe. They are also asked to describe events in the past, such as the outcome of Amelia Earhart's last flight, or a look inside a sealed container or locked room.

The goal of Distant-Sensing efforts is to receive signals and messages from the subconscious mind, with the help of our senses, and then interpret and decode that data to the Sensor's conscious mind. The signals are said to travel through the Sensor's subconscious mind and then into the sensor's consciousness, where it is deciphered into a form (verbally or materially) that can be reported clearly to others. Psychics with this ability are expected to actually view or *see* things without previous information or assistance. This is commonly referred to as being blind to the target.

The success of any Sense-Ability depends strongly on being used in tandem with other Sense-Abilities. It depends on the collective powers of other Sense-Abilities to obtain a complete mental impression. In short, the Distant Sensor relies on hearing the sounds surrounding the target and experiencing the tastes, smells, and textures vital to completely *seeing* the location, item, or event.

Distant Sensing also relies on the Sensor's interpretive skills for effective analysis and a comprehensive reporting of what he or she has seen. Once the Distant Sensor mentally interprets what he or she witnesses, he or she must convey that information to the client. It is not unusual for a Distant Sensor to be meticulously trained and to have a customized approach only he or she uses to conduct a complete a Distant Sensing transcript.

In her book *Harper's Encyclopedia of Mystical Paranormal Experience*, Rosemary Ellen Guiley, an American researcher and writer on topics related to spirituality and the paranormal, described Distant Sensing as, "Seeing remote or hidden objects clairvoyantly with the inner eye or through out-of-body travel." However, one does not need to travel out of body to learn this Sense-Ability. Anyone can learn this skill, and simply adhering to the structured process typically leads to successful identifying of the target location.

Distant Sensing is the most intriguing of the Sense-Abilities, not only because it requires a more intense and controlled use of one's psychic abilities but because it is the only Sense-Ability that has been the subject of scientific study by individuals, institutions, and the military. Studies involving psychic occurrences started in the mid-nineteenth century and predominately centered on testing individuals thought to have psychic abilities. The scientific community viewed those studies with extreme skepticism and eventually deemed the research methodology unscientific. However, in the 1930s, the research was reorganized and expanded to include large general populations and the use of standard scientific protocols. In spite of these improvements, paranormal research failed to produce repeatable results or positive peer reviews.

Things of the spirit are difficult to prove scientifically, but Distant Sensing remains a valid practice by those who have witnessed its results. Ingo Swann, an extraordinary psychic, artist, and author has been credited as the creator of the process of CRV (Distant Sensing). He is widely known for his work in paranormal research for the military venture known as the Star Gate Project. Swann refers to himself as a "consciousness researcher," who experiences "altered states of consciousness."

Swann developed CRV while working at the Stanford Research Institute in the early 1970s working in tandem with American physicists Russell Targ and Hal Puthoff. Swann's experiments with Distant Sensing caught the attention of the CIA. In *The Reality of ESP: A Physicist's Proof of Psychic Abilities*, Targ presents it was Swann who coined the term remote viewing and who also taught the army how to remote view.

On the evening of April 27, 1973, prior to the Voyager launch in 1979, Swann was involved in a blind CRV session, which resulted in his seeing the planet Jupiter and its moons. It took only three-and-a-half minutes for him to detect and describe its physical features. Swann described its surface, atmosphere, and weather. In his statement, he reported that Jupiter had planetary rings like Saturn, a controversial notion at the time. Later, the Voyager probe confirmed the existence of such rings. Swann's exact statement was, "Very high in the atmosphere there are crystals … they glitter. Maybe the stripes are like bands of crystals, maybe like rings of Saturn, though not far out like that … very close within the atmosphere. I bet you they'll reflect radio probes. Is that possible … if you had a cloud of crystals that were assaulted by different radio waves?"

Swann's Jupiter session was indeed remarkable, and his respected work in CRV certainly paved the way for like-minded researchers. Yet the results all reported paranormal research gleaned and reported during that time—governmental or otherwise—was deemed by the scientific community as unremarkable and unreliable. It was the inability of those targeted paranormal research projects to scientifically produce reliable results that brought projects to a halt. In recent years, however, with the introduction of credible organizations, like the International Remote Viewing Association (IRVA), we are seeing a major swing in a new direction. The scientific and research community is embracing Distant Sensing and other Sense-Abilities. There is a new wave of scientific researchers and independent thinkers sweeping the world, determined to prove there is more about our existence than we have yet discovered.

The negative pronouncements by the science community failed to dishearten the thousands of individuals and psychic practitioners who say they are witnesses to the remarkable outcomes of Distant-Sensing sessions of their own. For them, there is nothing to prove.

Distant Sensing is, by far, a more intense Sense-Ability than most of the others. It uses a person's *inner receptivity* as a vehicle for signals emitted by objects and places. Such receptivity is an indication that an object, which cannot be seen directly, is always available to one's subconscious mind because of its connection to the universal mind. These vibrations are also an exceptionally sophisticated benefit of ordinary intuitive realizations.

Distant Sensing, like all Sense-Abilities, requires one to limit any mental noise interfering with the execution of the psychic skill. This requirement is of utmost importance to the Distant Sensor. It is critical because mind chatter (thoughts regarding worldly concerns) that seeps into the Sensor's consciousness will prevent correct and authentic information from being recovered.

The process of Distant Sensing, as taught by psychic practitioners, involves training would-be Sensors to deal with and control the pollution and illegitimate imaginations often experienced in any intuitive process. It is one's inability to control *mind noise* that prevents a clear, undamaged extraction of information. It is important for the psychic instructor to introduce learners to systems and methodologies essential to effective Distant Sensing and that those instructors do so through a step by step process the learner can easily internalize. The instructor should guide the learner through sessions involving actual targets and progressively introduce more and more complex targets. He or she is expected to introduce methods and ideas to facilitate control of mental noise and outside distractions.

Distant Sensing is not a Sense-Ability that stands alone—unaided or disconnected from the other Sense-Abilities. It is a skill separate from clairvoyance and telepathy but needs the help of other Sense-Abilities to reach its full potential. In spite of the fact that Distant Sensors are highly trained and intuitive, anyone can learn their skills.

How Distant Sensing Is Used

- Locating missing people or objects
- Law enforcement cases
- In mining, locating things like minerals, water, etc.
- Accessing information about a person, place, or thing
- Seeing and recording an event in the past, present, or future
- Viewing inside inaccessible objects, like safes and locked rooms

- Visiting locations in the past

Upside-down Drawing and Right Brain Activity to Enhance Distant Sensing

It's natural for our left brain to be so in charge that you often can't regulate it. The following exercise will give your creative, intuitive right brain a chance to take over for a while. When you look at a photo right side up, you give it dimension and order. You see the top, bottom, sides, etc. It makes sense to your left brain. But if you look at that same picture upside down, suddenly it's chaos. Your brain can't make clear sense of it.

This is even more pronounced when you try to draw it upside down. Herein lay the doorway to opening your right brain. Follow these few steps, and you'll begin to nourish this remarkable, largely untouched side of who you are. For a more in-depth discussion on the intricacies of the right and left brain as they relate to drawing, consult *Drawing on the Right Side of the Brain* by Betty Edwards.

Here are the steps to follow:

1. Find a picture of a person you want to draw.
2. Get to a quiet place, and have at least thirty minutes of uninterrupted time. Choose a time and place where you can draw comfortably.
3. Turn the picture upside down, and begin drawing it on a clean sheet of paper. Start exactly where you feel you are led to start. There is no right or wrong place to begin. Don't try to figure out what you are drawing. Just draw what is before you. It's imperative that you don't turn the picture right side up, or you will shift back and awaken your left brain. You may want to cover what you are drawing with another piece of paper, and then gradually reveal sections of it as you draw, piece by

piece. This way, the picture and your progress will not seem overwhelming.

Healing the Body with Remote Viewing

Spiritual growth requires body, mind, and spiritual wholeness and balance. And, as strange as it may seem, it is possible to use remote viewing—Distant Sensing—to detect health issues and bring wholeness to one's body.

The first step is to hold the body as sacred and significant. Sports professionals consider health and having a high level of physical well-being a serious endeavor. Light-workers often use remote viewing to collect information from a client's past in order to convey that information to the client and help them heal emotionally, spiritually, and physically. Anyone can remote view to see any situation past, present, or future. He or she can use this skill to look for patterns and find the root cause of a health issue.

An athlete's routine involves practice, consistent training, rest, recovery, balanced nutrition, and routine hydration. The same is beneficial for the psychic. But remember: at the core of any endeavor is your spiritual self. Without an inner spiritual determination, any endeavor is doomed to failure. It's not an overstatement to say that your body is a temple, and you can do, be, or have anything you desire by remaining healthy in both body and spirit.

To begin work in Distant Sensing, quiet your mind; release left brain thoughts and mind chatter. Take a moment to ask, "What needs to be healed in my life?" In that moment, you will be taken to a time in your past when you experienced a situation of importance requesting your attention. The situation may be something from a past life. It may be a time of struggle or hardship that needs healing. It may be a childhood incident needing clarification and restoration. Or, it may be things from your recent past—behaviors you may need to change.

Closely observe everything that presents itself, and record it in as much detail as possible. With this kind of deep attention, there will likely be a surfacing of feelings or issues you have forgotten. You may find these to be extremely powerful impressions and feelings. Be an observer, but resist becoming immersed.

It is essential that you remain an observer because the thinking mind will try to recreate these emotions and feelings and become part of your identity. The issues you encounter are not your identity. They do not define you. You are not your experiences—ever. Rather, you are a witness. Disassociate with any overwhelming emotion. Learn from it instead. See it as on opportunity to heal and reconcile. Distant Sensing works to heal the mind, emotions, and body.

CHAPTER 17

PERSONAL GROWTH

I magine the power you would have to change lives if you could effectively practice any combination of the Sense-Abilities described herein. Imagine the changes you could initiate in yourself. Imagine the changes you could make in yourself if you could tap into the powers of your higher self. The changes, if possible, would be completely up to you.

Most individuals who seek the help and advice of a psychic come with questions they want answered. They also seek direction and reassurance. They come to a psychic because they believe the answers to their questions lie somewhere beyond themselves, and the problems they are experiencing seem so insurmountable they believe it will take the advice from the supernatural world to solve them.

After you have completed your training and begin working as a psychic and/or medium, you may find it important to add life coaching to your services. To do the best job you can as a psychic and to have the cooperation of the universal matrix requires that you inform the universe you have decided to be helpful, happy, and successful. Repeat those thoughts every day until you believe them. When you begin to believe them, the universe will cooperate with your decision.

All of us can testify to the fact that, to one extent or another we have been subject to a bit of programming in our lives—programming designed to keep us from doing what we were meant to do. Because of this, it is important to find a way to restructure your beliefs and programming in a way that will enable you to move forward in your chosen direction. As you move forward against old programming, you may feel resistance from within and from without. This is good because, when you feel you are going against the grain, it is quite possible your higher self is working with you. Your higher self will help you identify that the old way of doing things is no longer working for you. It may be the beginning of transferring into a new way of doing things. New things are always challenging and uncomfortable, but push on. Life always brings challenges, but your spirit has the capacity to evolve and learn from what you encounter on this earthly plane.

Each of us has a unique mental energy helping us make changes. In all the work you may do as a psychic, you will find you are able to help others find their own power. You will be able to help them realize they too have the tools and answers to conquer life's challenges and that the answers are within themselves.

Psychics may see mental images and psychic pictures ad infinitum, but if clients fail to realize that everything rests on how they think, nothing can be done. If clients do not realize the effect of failing to align themselves with their higher selves, the information they came for will not help. It is a psychic's job to reveal that truth.

CHAPTER 18

SPIRIT GUIDES

Spirit guides are entities designed to help and advise you on this physical plain of existence. Your guides—everyone has more than one—were given to you before you were made flesh. They are noncorporeal beings, assigned by the universal mind to travel alongside you while you exist on this earth. They are responsible for helping you navigate your way through life, expand your realization of your higher self, and make your journey easier. Spirit guides advise, nudge, comfort, and of course, guide. Their purpose is not to do things for you or make your decisions; they are there just to guide and inform. They are kindly entities, specifically concerned with your good—nothing more.

There are spirits of the departed, like loved ones who have passed on, engaged in helping and guiding, but they are not spirit guides. Spirit guides are different and should not to be confused with guardian angels or angels of any kind. The best explanation for spirit guides is to say they are entities, composed of energy, which do not have substance and which are often directed to aid your higher self.

Spirit guides are uniquely able to help where intuition is not. This is because spirit guides know all that has been and is now going on in your life. They are entities that may or may not work in concert with other guides on your behalf. They may appear to have male or female characteristics, but they are neither male nor female. Those characteristics are there to aid your human understanding and to give you something with which you can easily identify.

Spirit guides also communicate in a unique way. They come across through thoughts—strong thoughts. They send messages in the same way messages are sent to Spirit Interactors (mediums). Know that their connection with humans is always gentle. You should think about it as receiving a message unlike intuition or mental insight. It is stronger and more directed than that. The best way to think of spirit guide connections is to think of them as concerned messages with direction.

Spirit guide relationships are also unique. They are relationships you should cultivate as any other meaningful and important relationship requiring nurturing and caring. A spirit guide relationship needs the same level of commitment and time any significant relationship requires. The more time and attention you give to cultivating open lines of communication with your guide, the stronger your relationship will become.

Types of Guides

Best Friend Guide

Your best friend guide will be your main guide. It will be the one with whom you will spend most of your time and have most of your interaction. This guide is similar to a friend. It behaves like a companion, bringing comfort, laughter, and joy. It is around to remind you to handle situations with kindness and diplomacy. It is there to remind you to take a breath when things go wrong and to be patient with things difficult to change. This guide advises when choices involve your happiness. It is believed that this guide has lived a human life; because of this, it understands all you are experiencing and what the outcomes of decisions may be.

If you need a little boost to balance your day or to reignite your clarity of thought, your best friend guide is the one to help. If you find yourself a bit down about, expect your best friend guide to appear and prompt you to rethink your situation. It will remind you to laugh. Remember: your best friend guide is always present.

Guardian Guide

The job of your guardian guide is to keep you aware, forewarned, and safe. This guide often comes with messages of caution and warning. Think of the guardian guide as your chief protector. If you have a feeling cautioning you, it is probably your guardian guide, instructing you to be careful.

Wisdom or Scholar Guide

The wisdom or scholar guide is the teacher. If it were a being living on earth, it might take on the form of a wise old man with profound insights. It might be an individual with incomparable wisdom, whom you would find easy to trust.

If you have questions about learning, education, or philosophy, this is the guide who will assist you. It is the spiritual guru, versed in education and learning.

Body-Balance Guide

We have only one physical body, and it is sacred. The body-balance guide is concerned with your health and wellness—your diet, exercise, and medical care. If you hear a voice advising, "That is not a good choice for your body," listen. It is your body- balance guide giving you a nudge.

Short Term Guides

It is possible to ask the universe for short-term guides to help you. These are guides with a particular skill or information. If you are writing a book, then you may want to call on a guide skilled in that area. If you are preparing for a test, you may need a guide with expertise in that particular field of study.

All kinds of spirit guides, as helpful as they are, can't and won't make decisions for you. They're available only to assist you. There is a conundrum about the effectiveness of guides. Because we have a deep, intuitive knowledge about what is right for us and what is right to do, we don't always need a voice outside of ourselves—spirits, spirit guides, or anyone else—telling us what to do. But because human beings tend not to obey those things they know to be right, other entities often need to intervene to reinforce the necessity for doing what is right. Insecurity over a decision may not be valid. Dig deep within, and the choice will always be clear. Just remember to make choices that meld with your own goals and needs—not the goals and needs of others. The good news is that if you think you need the advice of a guide, you can have one whenever you choose.

How to Connect With Your Spirit Guides

- Set your intention to connect with your spirit guide.
- Sit in a relaxed, meditative state in a comfortable location. Meditation is where the profound, but remarkably gentle joining of you and your spirit guide will happen.
- Say a prayer to invite your guide to join you. You might say, "Spirit guide, thank you for coming. I intend accurate, open, clear lines of communication with you. I invite you into my space now."
- Listen and trust.

- Know that messages are subtle. Don't look for them. Let them float in naturally.
- Use your Sense-Abilities.
- Be consistent. Don't give up if messages from your guides don't present right away. This is a magnificently high vibrational relationship process. You and your spirit guides are adjusting to one another. It requires raising your vibrational frequency and lowering theirs. You will meet somewhere in the middle. It may require a few meditations before you have a clear awareness of your guides.

Naming Your Spirit Guide

People often ask, "How do I find my guide, and what is his or her name?" Connecting with spirit guides is done in several ways.

One is meditation. Meditation does not require any special training or insight. It is a simple process. Quiet your mind. When you feel you are substantially calm, ask your spirit guide to tell you his or her name. After you have asked, listen. Trust the first name that comes to your mind. That is the name of your guide. While some believe it is important to know the name of their spirit guides, others believe it has no relevance. Knowing your guide's name is not essential. The feelings and relationships you develop with your guide and the messages you receive are essential. Names are nothing more than a human system for identifying and connecting with people and things.

To identify whether or not a spirit is a guide, use the *three times* rule. If you receive the same message three times, it is a clue you are receiving guidance from a spirit guide. Pay attention to the repeated nudges and messages you receive, as your guides will send messages through those portals as well. You may feel it important to do something, and when the nudge occurs strongly three times, your guide is attempting to corral you in a certain direction. The reasons may be unclear to you at first, but your guide will make them obvious later. Use your Sense-Abilities to tune into your guide for support when you need it.

CHAPTER 19

EMOTIONAL ENERGY AND THE ROLE IT PLAYS

There are a number of tools learning psychics will add to their skill sets and services. One such skill is Matching Emotional Images (MEI). Most psychics employ MEI concepts as a way to think about a person's emotional life and the connections created between people, both good and bad.

Debra Lynne Katz is the founder and director of the International School of Clairvoyance. In her instructional book *You Are Psychic*, she has described MEI in the following way: "Mental/Emotional Image (MEI) pictures are concentrated pockets of emotional energy and corresponding thoughts, ideas, and beliefs that have accumulated in a certain location of our body" (Katz 61).

We all carry these *pockets* of emotional energy from events or suffering in our lives. They can be carried from previous lives as well. This accumulation of energy becomes associated with particular beliefs about who we are and the way the world works. These beliefs become so ingrained they influence our deepest beliefs, structure our relationships, and influence our perceptions of others. Psychics are particularly sensitive to these accumulations of emotion and energy and can access them in the form of mental images or pictures—MEI.

Whether these accumulations of emotion and energy are recent or whether they have been around since your earliest incarnations, they can be dangerous. If they go unacknowledged, they will create havoc with your emotional balance and your ability to function properly in the world.

The part of ourselves that is most affected by these emotional accumulations is self-esteem—our sense of who we are. We encounter people daily who have a particular picture of us because of their MEI issues. Absorption of the negative images of others adds to our own MEIs and may cause our true selves to suffer. Each negative relationship we encounter, whether through a friend, lover, or boss, leaves us feeling a little *less than*. As a result, these negative relationships reinforce our own worst ideas about ourselves and make it difficult to extricate ourselves from them. We invariably add their negative energies to our own and allow them to become part of our self-images. This process causes pockets of negative energy to build that a sensitive psychic or Visual Receptor can uncover. This person can see the pictures these energies conjure up, making us aware of their damage and helping us to dispel them.

Sometimes psychics are attracted to persons whose MEIs match their own. In other words, a psychic may be drawn to persons who share the same experiences, creating empathetic, negative energy pockets. It is also possible that matching pictures may resonate so intensively with the psychic that they serve to reinforce negative energies and cloud his or her ability to *see* clearly what needs to be done. This idea of matching pictures helps the psychic to aid a client in dispelling harmful beliefs and pictures. MEI energies can have a cumulative effect on one's physical body, but the real impact is on the mind and the spirit.

Another aspect of matching pictures is the tendency for someone to repeatedly attract the same kind of person into his or her life. When someone has a particular emotional block or accumulation, it may present itself as a pattern—a pattern in the choice of a harmful love interest or negative friendship. Those who succumb to this pattern are people who, no matter how painful a relationship, will choose and then tolerate those types of companions, simply because they match some erroneously held self-image. To rid one's self of such a pattern requires a true awareness of one's self-image and a desire to be rid of such a habit. Ridding one's self of falsely held images goes a long way towards attracting and keeping healthy relationships.

Bad images can reoccur, so you may need to cleanse your spirit of these maleficent energies several times before you are truly able to accept that your long-held belief about others or yourself is wrong. A psychic is a person aware of these issues, who can actively work to help you change them. Your training can also teach you how to change things.

While most MEIs are precursors to negative emotions, there are times when a kind of matching-picture therapy can be a good thing. Some experiences resonate with us on an emotional level, such as getting over a trauma. Matching pictures can help with these. It is possible for MEIs to happen in a conversation with someone you've just met or through something you've read in a book or through a movie you've seen. You may find yourself having a fierce reaction to one of these situations. Be patient as sometimes it will be difficult to determine which pictures were a match to you in those events. Psychic healers can often see these negative images. Skillful light-workers can also help to remove them.

However, if the self-image is so ingrained that it has become integral to a person's sense of self, it may be impossible to clear. If, over time, persons become polluted by pictures of themselves created by someone else or which were clouded by the result of a controlling event, the psychic needs to be aware of such information. Ridding one's self and others of these MEIs may be the most important facet of a practice.

In all these cases, it is better to make clients aware of the images, to point out the MEI, and to describe the picture with which they are being presented. Then, the psychic can let them decide how they want to deal with the situation. It is up to clients to relinquish those images or not. If they choose to relinquish them, strong determination will be required to send a message into the universe that they intend to change. They will have to send a powerful message of intention to establish a clean spiritual slate and let go of old, negative MEIs forever.

As a practicing psychic, you may find yourself in the presence of someone with whom you share matching pictures. It is crucial that you heed the warning about a pocket of energy within you that needs to be released. If you find yourself sharing similarities with a client, it's an indication you may have accumulated similar MEIs. Remember: all these images can take the form of belief systems or value judgments recurring throughout your life. Harsh judgment of others, intolerance, or indifference may be a sign you have acquired a pocket of negative energy that needs releasing.

Acknowledgment and awareness of the dangers of negative energy set the stage for resolving the problem. It is important to learn how to work with energy and cultivate a brave and honest attempt to know more about the areas of your personality.

We are all unique, and our paths are unique as well. But one thing is true; the more we tune into our own inner knowing, our emotions, and our awareness of where we are in the moment, the closer we will be to self-awareness and higher knowledge. All answers lie within you; that is the most powerful message of all. Tools, like meditation, will help you come closer to your authentic self and teach you to live in the moment. The future is something you create, at any moment, using your power of choice. Taking control of your life is where real happiness lies. It is in a complete awareness of yourself and an acceptance of the changes you may need to make. An honest effort goes a long way to ensure the progressive development of your psychic Sense-Abilities.

You may have curiosity about things of the higher mind, but you don't have a desire to become a psychic or make use of the skills necessary to become one. Everything mentioned in this book is intended to let you know there is more. It is intended to encourage you to be open to self-awareness and to show you the value of aligning yourself with who you really are.

We are all good at the core. We are made for joy and happiness. Life's circumstances may make that difficult to achieve. In some tragic cases, it's almost impossible, but everything can ultimately be managed with grace.

Individuals are often discouraged from embarking on a journey to explore their hidden psychic talents simply because such a practice is often mocked. This fear of retribution can lead to a failure in permitting spontaneous receptions or to discounting their authenticity.

Everyone encounters events or has receptive inclinations at one time or another, and you are no exception. The issue for you is whether or not the pursuit of psychic work is a calling and serious endeavor for you or only an area of casual interest. It is not important at this time to believe in anything at all. So don't be influenced by social norms or mainstream thinking. If you have an innate curiosity or a predisposition to all things psychic, it is enough. Judge for yourself the quality of your potential involvement and interest.

When developing your receptive psychic Sense-Abilities (regardless of which ones you choose to explore), your focus should be on understanding the process and researching the techniques needed to expand them. It is necessary to approach your learning with an open mind, realizing you will not always have the answers or know exactly what has happened. The universal mind and your connection to it are complex. What is important is for you is to become astute at identifying when a psychic phenomenon is happening and when it is not.

In spite of the fact that you are psychic in some way, and some of your Sense-Abilities may be more developed than others, it is important to recognize that the right training and techniques are necessary to maximize any Sense-Ability.

From the time you embark on this quest, take notice of every possible psychic encounter that happens in your day to day living. Note that psychic receptions can be triggered when you are researching who you are. Take note of your energies or any unusual connections or happenings you may have previously discounted. Attempt to put them in a psychic context, or try your hand at interpreting what you have experienced. Your innate abilities will direct you to a particular path or conclusion.

Remember: the hidden power residing in the psychic realm is available to those who recognize and accept a higher state of knowing— something beyond their own physical bodies. The universe is full of this power. It is energy that can be tapped by anyone who makes the effort to tune in to the vibrations emanating from it. Focus is the key. Without focusing on the signs and energies of the universe, it is difficult to recognize psychic events.

Take it upon yourself to focus on this power and its energies. Join a development circle, where people with the same intentions and hopes can practice in a nonjudgmental environment, where you can explore your aptitude. You can also connect with a professional psychic for guidance and instruction to ensure you are gauging things correctly and walking along the right path.

Your first steps must include a few common, necessary skills that are especially important to acquiring psychic Sense-Abilities: relaxation and concentration. It may seem simple, but our modern lifestyle often makes relaxation and concentration into a formidable hill to climb. You should learn to relax to the extent that your mind no longer pays attention to your physical body. Yoga, Thai Chi, and meditation techniques can help to relax your mind and body at will.

Relaxation techniques will enable you to tune into the universe, without the stress and burden of day to day events blocking the connection. You are so designed that you can change and grow into a making of your own design and structure. You are energy, living and functioning in a physical body. You can only take advantage of this gift if you insist on not being distracted by the mundane events surrounding you. Concentration is often more difficult than relaxation, although it is almost impossible to concentrate unless one is relaxed enough to focus. Relax and then train yourself to concentrate, to focus on the skills you want to acquire.

Learning about Energy

There are three types of energy: auric energy, cosmic energy, and earth energy.

Auric energies

Auric energy is energy generated by conscious, thinking human beings. It is the energy we know as aura. Humans are a combination of soul (auric) energy, earth energy, and cosmic energy. Psychics call this personal energy combination a PSI signature.

Cosmic Energies

Cosmic energy exists in the cosmos. Cosmic energy is energy generated by the universal mind. It is the force that functions throughout the universe. It is the energy in charge of universal order and chaos. Psychics often visualize this energy as a warm, peaceful, white light. It is an energy infinite in nature but easy to detect and identify. This is the energy we acquire when we refer to feeling energized, invigorated, or rejuvenated.

Earth Energies

Earth energies are those energies emanating from the core of the planet and Mother Nature. This energy is present in every stone, tree, or blade of grass. It is in every plant and every animal. It is energy psychics use to ground themselves when they perform any type of energy work. It is the energy found in the nucleus of an atom, in the force of thunder, in the feeling of the air. Everything in the universe is comprised of this energy—energy that flows naturally, without constraints.

Which Energies Do Psychics Use?

Humans are always making use of all three energies. We use them without being aware we are using them. It is part of our daily routine, like using cosmic energy when we sleep to re-energize or bodies and minds.

Psychics also use all three energies. But they use them in a deliberate way and with a conscious knowing. If you are an empath, you may be taking advantage of auric energies to connect with people, earth energies to receive messages from your surroundings, and cosmic energy to transfer information via telepathy. Acknowledging and accepting the forces of energy are essential to being a psychic. They are essential to develop the power of your psychic connections and to strengthen your overall Sense-Abilities.

CHAPTER 20

THE DISCOURAGING EFFECTS OF FEAR

J oy is what we all hope will be recorded in how we lived and experienced our lives. Joy makes living easy, comfortable, and pleasurable. However, joy can be thwarted by one controllable emotion—fear—fear of all kinds. Fear of criticism, particularly, has the power to keep us from being who we are and doing what we want to do. It is the one emotion that can keep us from making decisions essential for a life of joy and happiness.

Fear of criticism is the granddaddy of all fears because it prevents us from doing those things we know, in our hearts, we should be doing. Fear of criticism forces us to opt for the unsatisfying choices others tell us are nobler, nicer, or just plain better. Fear of criticism also makes it impossible to clearly define what we want for ourselves and for others who are important to us.

Those who accept someone else's choices are bound to fail. They learn to make excuses for that failure and may become habitual procrastinators. Individuals who fear criticism take on these behaviors because they are fighting life choices they did not make; they feel forced to behave in ways they did not choose. Procrastination and excuses are feeble alternatives to just saying no. Instead of opting for doing the things to make their own lives shine, fear victims search for compromises that please others instead of themselves.

Fear is also the enemy of a truly psychic experience. It prevents those wanting to become psychics from performing their best. Fear is the foundation of tunnel vision, faulty perceptions, and faulty judgments, all of which are antithetical to the clear, unhampered tasks psychics perform. Psychics must be open and honest to ensure the clarity of the messages they receive, for the sake of the people they serve. If openness is limited by something as controllable as fear, the practice of any Sense-Ability will be less effective and, in extreme cases, invalid. There can be no success at anything without willingness to take a chance on something new and courage to stare fear in the face.

Debilitating, success-destroying fear includes the fear of failure. When attempting to practice your newfound psychic skills, it is important to *fire the committee.* The committee is an imaginary group, made up of all the people you imagine are standing behind you, judging you, and correcting you. The committee speaks with imaginary voices only you can hear. The thought process of committee members may or may not be the reality you imagine it to be. So, when embarking on your practice as a psychic, remember to ignore the committee, and just do your best. The cure for failure: practice and determination.

It is quite common for beginners to feel strong insecurities, that messages sent from the universal matrix are misunderstood. They may fail to make an effective connection and later realize no message was actually sent. New practitioners must be patient with their learning processes and internalize the fact that no skill is executed effectively without time, practice, patience, study, and confidence.

One thing necessary for getting past any fear is to acknowledge that fear panders to ego. We must be prepared to ignore ego and see things as they truly are, without the fog of fear. Ego prevents growth, opting instead to protect what we have and don't want to lose. Ego is a false sense of self-protection. Remember: fear is a closed door that makes it impossible to achieve success in any undertaking. Check your ego and proceed in spite of your fears.

CHAPTER 21

SENSE-ABILITIES AND ALTERED STATES OF CONSCIOUSNESS

M*erriam Webster's Dictionary* defines altered state of consciousness as a medical term, meaning "any of the various states of awareness (sleep, dreams, drug-induced hallucinogenic states, or a trance) that deviates from, and is usually clearly demarcated from ordinary waking consciousness."

However, there are other definitions of this term, and those definitions come from the psychic experience. Psychics believe it is impossible to reduce the idea of consciousness to the confines of an intellectual awareness of the physical world. Mystics and seers the world over have spoken of otherworldly states of consciousness for hundreds of centuries. Normal consciousness is earth-bound and is only normal in the sense that it is well known. This *normal* form of consciousness is neither good nor bad; it just is.

Our current understanding of consciousness is rigid and fails to give recognition to the conscious experiences outside the definition of normal. Such experiences are considered fake, abnormal, or unnatural. One such altered state is the trance. Mediums often experience a dissociative condition, a trance-like state of consciousness when they are communicating with spirits. Hypnosis is another form of a conscious state not fitting normal definitions. Another is the drug-induced state used by shamans or medicine men and women for obtaining information, relating events, or diagnosing illnesses and suggesting cures.

Yoga and Zen practitioners believe that all meditative traditions are associated with the development of paranormal powers. We can even go so far as to say that night dreams are actually an altered state of consciousness, to which we give little credit.

Precognition comes as the result of an altered state of consciousness. Night dreams, hypnosis, and meditation are all methods frequently used by psychics. Messages are transmitted through dreams, focused contemplation (meditation), and other ESP functions. These altered states are made possible by deliberating quieting the body, mind, and senses. Doing so opens the psychic to images, thoughts, and feelings not common to others. Seemingly abnormal states of consciousness ignore the internal and external distractions apparent in normal states of consciousness. Psychic impressions, bombarded by sensory noise and mental distractions, prevent the kind of altered states of consciousness possible when distractions don't intervene. In other words, the world is reluctant to recognize other altered states of consciousness, but psychic practitioners have accepted, honored, and used them to reach beyond the physical world.

CHAPTER 22

SUPER-CONSCIOUSNESS

The subconscious mind is not mysterious to us. We are familiar with it in our everyday lives. We experience it when we sleep, dream, and behave according to beliefs we are not aware we have. The same thing is true of our conscious minds. We have no trouble acknowledging we are alive, making decisions, and thinking every waking moment. However, unfamiliar to us is a third consciousness— super-consciousness.

Super-consciousness is the hidden spiritual system behind intuition, spirituality, and physical and spiritual healing. Super-consciousness is responsible for problem-solving and our capacity to feel such things as joy, excitement, and empathy. The work of our super-consciousness is often overlooked when we aspire to live a richer, more meaningful life.

Though we are familiar with fleeting moments of raised consciousness and enlightenment, few know the technique for purposely entering the exalted state of super-consciousness. It is a state that can only be reached through meditation, chanting, affirmation, and prayers designed specifically to help acquire super-consciousness.

Swami Kriyananda, widely recognized as one of the world's foremost authorities on meditation and yoga, is someone who teaches methods for reaching super-consciousness regularly, successfully, and with maximum beneficial effect. In his book *Awaken to Superconsciousness,* Kriyananda reveals ancient yoga traditions and practices essential to learning how to reach inner peace through super-consciousness. *Awaken to Superconsciousness* provides a comprehensive, easy-to-understand program. It is designed to assist in tapping into your own wellspring of creativity, unlocking your intuitive guidance, and enhancing your ability to hear the largely silent voice of your soul.

Bridge to Superconsciousness, a book by Rick Prater who is a leading expert in meditation practice, outlines a process of spiritual development for reaching higher levels of consciousness in daily life and for living in a more enlightened way. It affirms the greatness of human potential and shows how to realize that potential through individual and group work.

The idea of a higher consciousness is rooted in the notion of reaching the higher self, the transcendental reality, and the universal spirit. It is the essence of human existence, capable of going beyond the confines of the physical world, perceived realities, and the trappings of logic.

In his book, *The Spectrum of Consciousness,* American writer and philosopher, Ken Wilber describes consciousness as a scale, with ordinary awareness at one end and deep sentience at the other.

CHAPTER 23

YOUR HIDDEN TALENT

I t is common for us to have talents of which we are unaware. We may not acknowledge what talents we have or belittle them as unimportant and insignificant. But if we are honest with ourselves and take a good look at who we are, we would be forced to admit that we are exceptional at one thing or another. We may not be working with those talents or using them to make a better life for ourselves, but they are there, and we know what they are.

Talents often show themselves through hobbies or avocations. For example, while a person may be employed as a bookkeeper, that same person may spend an inordinate amount of time learning and researching history. Years of pursuing this interest have made him or her expert in the field of history. The person may not assign the word *expert* to what he or she knows, but it is still expertise. It is usually those things we love to do (and would do without pay) that manifest as talents. We are usually endowed with more than one such talent.

The same is true of psychic talents. You have already been introduced to your psychic talents. They are already yours. You only have to take time to notice what they are. Pay attention to everything that happens to you, and be mindful of your responses. Become acquainted with any inkling you may have regarding your psychic abilities. Read about them, and investigate what they mean to you. Learn where you feel most comfortable and where you may fit in. Attempt to allow any psychic tendencies to manifest, without judgment or preconceived notions. Clear your mind, and manage your emotions. Allow yourself to be skeptical, and then rationally evaluate whether or not you have the mindset or knack to be a psychic.

To truly find your path in life, you have to be investigative. You have to look at what you want and what rings true for you. In your probing, your emotions will always guide you correctly. They are the best compass system you have. Trust them. Adopt a determination to identify your talents. Then, practice them, understand them, and develop them. You may identify a talent or a way of viewing things that isn't identified in the same way by others. Your talents may present in ways that don't happen for anyone else.

The most important thing in the acquisition of Sense-Abilities is belief. One has to believe such things are possible in order for them to be true and manifest. Truth and reality are concepts to be weighed in any attempt to pursue a life course. And, as Shakespeare said through the character of Polonius, "This above all: to thine own self be true, And it must follow, as the night the day, Thou canst not then be false to any man."

CHAPTER 24

THE NECESSITY OF PROTECTION

While there is much that is positive about working with psychic Sense-Abilities, there are areas of caution. It is essential and compulsory that, when delving into the world of psychic phenomena, you recognize the need for spiritual, mental, and physical protection. Protection must be considered, not only for yourself but for the safety of your loved ones. There are, we regret to say, spirits of lower vibration, whose only reason for existing is to spread chaos and turmoil. They are spirits that want nothing more than to bring negative energy and negative situations into your life and surroundings.

It is important to know, when you are dealing with spirits or working to connect with them, there are good spirits and not so good spirits. The difficulty inherent in this situation is that you may not always know (at least right away) with which type of spirit you are dealing. You won't know the intention of a spirit until you make contact with it. Even if your goal is to connect with a spirit you already know is good, it is possible that a lower vibration spirit will intervene.

As you proceed along your path of universal connections and higher planes of existence, you will be more aware of the myriad of spiritual energies around you. You will be exposed to new realms of being, and as a consequence, you will become more sensitive to their vibrations. This increase in awareness will bring increased vulnerabilities. Therefore, it is necessary for you to create a safe space, where positive energy can dwell and negative energy is forbidden.

Practicing psychics develop a protection rose or a prayer of protection to send a message to the universe of their strong intentions to be protected. A prayer of protection is personal and is often repeated aloud. Its power is in the strong intention of the practitioner. It is a prayer said before starting the day and before any reading or energy work takes place.

While a protection prayer is a verbal expression—alerting negative spirits to keep their distance—a protection rose is a meditative energy tool that reinforces a clear boundary against negative energy. It acts as a filter to prevent energies not your own from accessing your space. It is a defense mechanism to ensure safe and protected sessions.

To create a protection rose, you must first envision a rose clearly in your mind's eye. See the colors and smell the aroma. See the beauty of it from the ground up, along the green stem, onto the shape and texture of the leaves, to the actual shape and form of the rose petals. The vision of your rose, and the pure essence of energy it imparts, will invade your space, protecting you with a strong, unfettered connection to the universe. Your mind cannot tell the difference between reality and imagination. Because of that, the unencumbered vision of your rose actively acts as your energy protector. The universe will honor your effort and your intention to be protected.

It doesn't take long for you to establish a daily routine of envisioning your rose and employing the vision before you enter a session. Take the time and be safe. Remember that any routine is an ongoing process that only becomes a habit with practice and consistency.

Steps to Create a Protection Rose

1. Envision a vibrant, colorful rose, and make it any color you desire.
2. Make it as tall and wide as you are.
3. Place it just outside your aura.
4. Ground it to the center of the earth.
5. State your intention for the rose to act as a filter to keep pure, positive energy in your space and to keep other energies in their spaces.

CHAPTER 25

LEARNING TO BE IN THE CENTER OF YOUR HEAD

Staying in the center of your head is just as important as being focused and clear. Our lives are full of significant experiences, and psychic experiences elevate that significance. The nature of what psychics do means they will invariably have episodes in which they will assume the emotions of a client or fall into the chaos of an event.

As a practicing psychic, you are bound to come face to face with highly-charged experiences, despite protective precautions. More often than not, the reason will be an inability to keep your attention focused outside of yourself. If you don't stay focused, you will become entrenched in whatever situation is emotionally overactive at the moment. The solution to this problem is to consistently be in the center of your head, to call back your life force, and to regain your peace of mind—your clarity and balance.

There is a spiritual space in the center of your head, from which you will be able to filter out worldly circumstances and focus on controlling the intensity of your experiences. The center of your head is a place of balance and perspective. It is a place for you and only you. It is comparable to being in a spiritual cocoon. Think of this place as a personal inner space, offering you a bird's-eye view of the reality of a situation. It can be place of peace, equanimity, and clarity. Maintaining an existence at the center of your head should be an ongoing process. It's not something done once. Your ability to remain centered is important to your stability and growth.

Steps to Stay in the Center of Your Head

1. Focus your awareness on the center of your head.
2. Imagine a miniature version of yourself located at the midpoint, the point where two crossed lines, traveling through the center, meet.
3. Take time to create a mental picture of this sacred space exactly as you choose. It is your space to design and arrange any way you wish.
4. Imagine a trap door. If persons or issues invade your space, tell them to leave. Then, imagine their immediate evictions. Remember: the center of your head is your sacred place. You control it, and you are responsible for keeping it free of negativity.

CHAPTER 26

HOW DO I KNOW MY PRACTICES ARE WORKING?

The short answer is, you will know. Identifying psychic ability isn't rocket science, and like any inborn talent, your abilities are already at work. You don't have to follow complicated routines, rituals, and belief systems or pledge your undying loyalty. If you think you exhibit psychic abilities, you probably do. The only job you have is to identify whether or not those abilities go above and beyond the ordinary. You decide when, how, and to what extent you will use your abilities.

Research on the subject of psychic skills may lead you to believe that pursuing a career or avocation as a psychic is a complicated, long-distance run to the finish line. The simple truth is any raw talent requires training. While a person may have been born with a talent, it takes professional training to make the most of that talent. Famous artists and musicians had mentors, teachers, or served as apprentices. Training is giving innate talent over to study. It is talent that becomes a skill. Your major concern should be how to take a rational approach to experiencing everything psychic, and determine whether or not such experiences are for you.

Ask yourself the following questions:

- Do I pay attention to my random thoughts and feelings? Have I begun to see connections as something bigger and more important?
- Is my overall awareness of people increasing? Is my awareness of emotions and spirit increasing? Am I noticing the possible implications of something more attached to an object?
- Am I more aware of my surroundings—its sights, sounds, textures, and smells?
- Do I find myself working to discover which psychic abilities I may or may not have?
- Do I spend quiet time meditating and contemplating what exists beyond the reality of this world?
- Do I realize that small, seemingly insignificant things are things from which to learn?

If you can say yes to any of these questions, your psychic abilities are at work. If you are not sure of your abilities, don't despair. Take no notice if you feel unsure or if you aren't making quick progress. You may not be aware of the benefit of what you are doing or the impact you are having on others. You may be the victim of a misguided focus or a false belief about your influence and your gifts. Take time to find a quiet place, where you can safely evaluate the insights you acquire and the possible quality of your psychic talents. Think about what everything means and what is pointing you in a particular direction. Be patient with yourself, concentrate on your sensory attunement, and be aware of the quality of your energy output.

Benefits of Developing Psychic Sense-Abilities

The practice of any Sense-Ability gives you access to other dimensions, as well as an enormous responsibility. Psychic Sense-Abilities enable each practitioner to understand situations from a broader perspective. The development of Sense-Abilities is not unlike learning other skills. It may be difficult at first, but it gets easier as you develop your expertise and become more proficient.

There is a lot to sort out when you embark on a program to engage and work with your psychic Sense-Abilities. A clear, theoretical base and practical techniques will help to focus your efforts. You will have to practice techniques and look into proposed theories. You will need to learn to relax and relax on cue, making it easier for you to pick up nonphysical cues too subtle for beginners to detect.

Here are some benefits you can expect from your psychic experiences:

- Less stress and less anxiety
- More creativity
- Forecast of what's ahead
- Improved relationships
- Increased concentration
- Better decision making
- Increased discernment
- Enhanced connectivity with the universal matrix

CHAPTER 27

SPIRIT CIRCLES

A spirit circle can be a first step for those of you who believe your Sense-Abilities point to formal psychic or mediumship work or for those who simply have a desire to expand learning and explore the topic more. Like any gathering of like minds, a spirit circle is a formal meeting of individuals wishing to become more proficient at a skill or to expand their knowledge base. In the case of a spirit circle, the skills are psychic in nature, and the knowledge base is the development of a clearer, more substantial connection with the universal mind and the spirits inhabiting other spiritual planes.

Those who participate in spirit circles, usually a group of seven to ten individuals, collectively want to gain additional knowledge of the spirit world and expand beyond the confines of the physical world. They want to do these things directly and comprehensively.

Spirit circles exist fundamentally to practice psychic skills. A spirit circle is not a place for lectures or formal instruction. It is a sacred and safe space to evolve and grow in spirituality. It is best thought of as a channeling or a reading or a spiritual sitting. Individuals who comprise a spirit circle are generally there to exchange energies and participate in one or more psychic Sense-Abilities. Group members determine the actual procedures followed. Some circles open by contacting spirit guides or by asking loved ones to be present. Others may begin with a short meditation period and then work to come into tune with each other's wavelengths.

The goal of all circle members is to expand their own spiritual awareness and their ability to receive messages coming from the universal matrix. Circle members also want to obtain a better connection to their higher-selves.

Some circles participate in contacting spirits in order to obtain messages pertinent to someone in the group. Others conduct healing sessions to revitalize the spiritual connections of its members. No matter what the function of any particular group, each spirit circle or energy exchange has, at its core, the goal of going beyond the barriers of life, death, time, space, and location.

If the idea of a spirit circle causes you skepticism, it is best to wait before you attempt to participate. Nonbelievers hinder the effectiveness of a circle and work as an interfering energy.

For those who believe, a spirit circle can be important to their development. A circle's aim is two-fold: personal and spiritual growth. All members have a common goal: the development of mental, emotional and spiritual faculties. A circle promotes the expansion of one's ability to think and reason, one's discernment, and one's ability to understand the human soul and its relationship to universal energies.

It is essential for those participating in a spirit circle to first have a strong understanding of how energy works—something that is also foundational to getting the most out of the experience. Circle members can benefit from the spiritual interaction with each other by learning about each other's challenges, practicing together, and sharing each other's progress. Such sharing accelerates spiritual growth to a point difficult to achieve alone. Circle members benefit from the collective energy generated by the members, as well as the energy of their individual spirit guides.

CHAPTER 28

HOW TO GET STARTED

Once you've accepted the idea of a higher realm—that world is not just what you see—you will be free to explore everything that means. And, if you believe as Shakespeare wrote, "There are more things in heaven and earth … than are dreamt of in your philosophy," then you should consider learning more.

The universe is full of energy, available to anyone who wants to tune in to its subtle vibrations. These vibrations, like energy, are available to those who make the effort to learn. If learning more is your intention, focus is required to activate the forces. Concentrate and evaluate even the smallest instances of psychic phenomena that happen in your life and the lives of others. Become familiar with the ethereal forces involved and how those forces integrate to exhibit hidden powers in action.

One of the most important things to learn is the philosophy that everything is connected—plants, animals, people, and the universe. This knowledge will give you a different perspective on life and the claim that there is a connection between the living and the dead. Understanding this concept is necessary for developing your latent psychic ability.

Once you adopt psychic philosophies, the next thing to do is to develop a new mindset. See happenings as more than random, as more than collected coincidences. Then, examine what your gifts are. Pay attention to how the universe sends information your way. It is quite possible that you already have inklings as to the particular psychic talents you have. Test those talents. Practice them to become proficient. Each person endeavoring to engage in psychic practices has a different set of talents; identify which ones are yours.

Learn the principles psychics are known to live by. Diligently apply yourself to accomplish the exercises given you by a trainer, and make use of the instructions you have gleaned from your personal research. Test the quality of your newly-acquired skills by practicing them. Look for a way to obtain continuous feedback on your progress and an objective assessment of your skills. A professional trainer will provide that and will guide your growth. The most important requirement to fully develop your latent abilities is to accept the foundational concept that there is more to the world than we suspect or see.

The next important requirement is to have a desire and willingness to develop psychically to the extent you are able to connect with the universal mind. Listen to what the spirit has to say, and honestly deliver that information. Don't forget that meditation facilitates every connection. It also opens the channels to your Sense-Abilities and the role you will play in the lives of others. Meditation will go a long way towards speeding your psychic development.

Things to Remember

- Your psychic journey is unique and highly individual. It is important to honor that.
- Report what you see, regardless of what it is, even if it seems ridiculous or silly. Too often, individuals new to practicing their Sense-Abilities are afraid to say what they see and fail to recognize it as feasible. In so doing, they lose meaningful

information. What you receive from the universe or the spirits always has meaning.

- As you begin practicing your psychic abilities, trust images and impressions you *first* encounter because what you first encounter will probably be most accurate. What comes first is correct.

- You are the boss. Use your own higher knowing and intuition, and listen to your inner voice. They provide the most valuable information you can get, so trust it. Your emotions and gut feelings are part of this intuitiveness.

- Relax. Enjoy the journey. It is a process, and the process is the gift. Your psychic development should be done in fun!

- Let psychic information come to you. You need not force it or search it out. Your desire to be right or *get* the images you intend is ego speaking. Ego hinders your connection.

- Be rooted in ethics and integrity. All your readings, healings, intuitive abilities, and other modalities are practiced with the permission of the person you are helping.

CHAPTER 29

HOW TO CHOOSE A PSYCHIC TRAINING COURSE OR TEACHER

Choosing an avenue for focusing and directing your psychic leanings is neither complicated nor elaborate. It begins with acknowledging the fact that, no matter what you want to do, some form of skilled instruction and training must be involved. There is no occupation or profession, whether or not you have an exalted talent for it, which does not require learning. A talent, inclination, or a wish to become something is not an end in itself. You must take whatever talent you have and build upon that foundation a fortress of skill and knowledge.

Vincent van Gogh did not wake up one morning and decide he was going to be an artist and create a new method of painting. He learned the basics of drawing and composition in elementary school, later studied at the Royal Academy of Art in Brussels, and thereafter, exchanged insights and ideas with Impressionists such as Claude Monet, August Renoir, Edgar Degas, Alfred Sisley, Paul Signac, Georges Seurat, and the Pissarro brothers, Lucien and Camille. This is how he learned what he might become in the world of painting, how to expand his creativity, how to explore his art, and how to become a painter with an identity all his own.

To embark on a path of learning more about psychic skills, philosophies, and realities, you must do your homework. Because psychic guidance is different from any other type of learning, it is important for you to find the right person or institution for training purposes. It is not the same as looking for an academic college or instructor. In this instance, your choices will not only affect what you learn but how you will practice. Your choices should ultimately give you the opportunity to achieve your expectations. But remember: no choice is permanent. You can always change or add to your choice at any time.

The first thing to consider when searching for psychic training is to give thought to who you are and under what conditions you thrive. Are you more apt to flourish with directive, subjective, or collaborative teaching? Consider your schedule, the impact on your family, and the amount of time involved in a particular type of training. Consider also your learning style. Do you learn best by doing, hearing, or seeing?

A directive teacher concentrates on presenting, clarifying, and standardizing information. He or she concentrates on the gleaning of facts, showing you what to do, and demonstrating how to do it.

Nondirective instructors focus on active listening behaviors and paraphrasing information. They encourage students to question and reach their own solutions, while encouraging them to analyze what and why they are learning.

Collaborative teaching is a third kind of instruction. It primarily involves the processes of problem solving, brainstorming, compromising, teamwork, sharing, and mutual goal setting.

Take your time. Get recommendations. Look at the achievements and writings of the teacher you are considering. Everything you learn about a teacher will tell you something about his or her commitment, interests, and perceived responsibility. It may also be helpful for you to audit a class before you make a commitment. Visit the location. Use your intuition and psychic perceptions to evaluate how you feel about every piece of information you acquire. Even things like the location will speak to you. You will have emotional sensations connected to everything, giving you an inclination of whether you fit in with a particular school or not.

Once you start your research, you will have an array of choices. Psychic instructors can be found everywhere on the Internet. Read their websites for clues as to their method, direction, and underlying philosophy. Write down the five most important things you believe will make you a successful student.

Above all, you will want to make sure the teaching encourages innovative ways to discover hidden aspects of yourself, your spirit, and your innate spiritual leanings. Your instruction should touch on exciting ways to experience your abilities, as well as techniques for releasing unconscious fears standing in the way of your spiritual progress. Good teachers will be trained to recognize their own ego tendencies and subjugate them to allow students to shine and thrive. It is never about the teacher; it is about the work.

Learning can be challenging. Students constantly face conceptual, social, emotional, and mental obstacles. You may need to find a teacher who has walked a path similar to yours, with psychic abilities similar to yours. Know that good teachers are always and only invested in your progress. They see their training efforts as an extension of their own ongoing learning. They see them as an arm of their spiritual practice, not as a financial goal or a personal expression of themselves. They see their jobs as a calling, not an opportunity to exercise control over others.

CHAPTER 30

IN CONCLUSION

There are things in the world we can't understand. All around us, things function without explanation or permission. Even the sun rises and sets without our input and would do so whether or not we were around to see it. There are concepts we can't explain: unconditional love, devotion, honesty, and sacrifice. If we are serious about making the most of our lives here on earth, we will endeavor to find and be our truest selves. We will crave a soul that is pure, kind, and considerate. We will want to pay homage to things like honor and integrity—concepts and ideals growing within us, concepts life is urging us to seek. We often strive for good, not always knowing how to achieve it.

This book is not intended to be the answer to these unknowns. It is written merely to tell you what could be. Who we are and what concepts we choose to worship or honor are totally within our capacities as humans to claim.

Whatever choice you make about aligning yourself with a philosophy, you should make it with seriousness and forethought. Throughout your life, you will be arming yourself with knowledge, but you will also be aligning yourself with a belief structure. Anything that calls you to believe (not just know) requires deep thought. You will be making a commitment affecting how you live, how you guide others, and how you approach the sacred things of life.

I have taken time to introduce you to another way of thinking, another way of being, and another realm of reality. Take from this book what speaks to you, and use the information as a tool to enhance your life. If what has been discussed here resonates with you, use the information to find a new and more expansive you.

NOTES

NOTES

NOTES

NOTES

NOTES

NOTES

NOTES

NOTES

NOTES

NOTES

ABOUT THE AUTHOR

Michelle A. Beltran is a psychic medium, author, and intuitive life coach. She has become a leading international authority in the spirituality arena, specializing in psychic functioning, spiritual counseling, and mediumship. She is the owner of *Readings with Michelle, LLC.*

Michelle has studied under internationally known instructors at the nation's top psychic training schools. She has used her gift of intuition and insight to help everyday people, entrepreneurs, thought leaders, therapists, professional athletes, CEOs, students, doctors, lawyers, celebrities, housewives, teachers, and others who are seeking to understand life and live it wholeheartedly. She recognizes that all of us seek to perfect our own humanity and to achieve lives that honor the soul.

Her life began in Northern California, where she grew up and attended elementary, high school, and college. She earned a bachelor's degree in political science and soon after was encouraged by her father to seek a career as a law enforcement officer. While in the United States Air Force, she traveled throughout the United States and Far East and often found herself thrust into situations requiring her to manage things in an alternatively authoritative and tactful manner. As a probation officer working in different social situations, she learned to deal with human problems in a way which demanded new approaches. She came to realize there is more to the human condition than she formerly assumed. This gave her insight and understanding into the needs of different individuals, their personalities, and problems. She came to know that human beings are not only capable of great change, but they also have an infinite capacity for achievement.

A former professional cyclist and lifelong fitness enthusiast, Michelle finds much of the clairvoyant information she receives is about nutrition, health, and fitness. She credits her experience of participating in a competitive sport with her gift for medical intuitiveness that she now shares with clients. She marvels at her unforgettable experiences racing abroad with the *Giro Italia with Forno d' Asolo* international cycling team, as well as two invitations to the US National Development Team Camp at the Olympic Training Center in Colorado Springs, Colorado.

"Professional cycling brings a never-ending growth process, much like that of being a psychic," says Michelle. "I believe deeply that balancing health and nutrition promotes vitality and psychic intuitiveness."

Psychic talents are to be cherished, and Michelle values the wonderful ability she has to see beyond chaos and unravel the best *next step* for her clients. She is lauded for her accuracy and her ability to tune in to situations. She is happy to provide direction necessary for her clients' greatest well-being.

Michelle's sessions are unique in that they provide guidance and serve to teach others how to stand in their own power. Her sessions teach clients how to access their higher knowing, intuitive gifts, and their connections to spirit. Whether clients are endeavoring to work through a relationship, change a career, or make a business decision, Michelle employs all of her psychic gifts to help them see what is next for their lives.

Made in the USA
Columbia, SC
24 September 2017